FOUNDING FEDERALIST

LIVES OF THE FOUNDERS

EDITED BY JOSIAH BUNTING III

FOUNDING FEDERALIST

THE LIFE OF OLIVER ELLSWORTH

Michael C. Toth

WILMINGTON, DELAWARE

Library of Congress Cataloging-in-Publication Data

Toth, Michael C.
    Founding federalist : the life of Oliver Ellsworth / Michael C. Toth.
    p. cm.
    Includes bibliographical references and index.
    ISBN 978-1-61017-147-2

    1. Ellsworth, Oliver, 1745–1807. 2. Judges—United States—Biography. 3. United States. Supreme Court—Biography. 4. Statesmen—United States—Biography. 5. Revolutionaries—United States—Biography. I. Title.

KF8745.E4T68 2011
347.73'2634—dc23
[B]
    2011019375

ISI Books
Intercollegiate Studies Institute
3901 Centerville Road
Wilmington, DE 19807-1938
www.isibooks.org

Manufactured in the United States of America

To Dad, in memory

CONTENTS

Author's Note:

Unless the original usage is easily recognizable, the spelling and punctuation of all quotations have been modernized.

PREFACE

Oliver Ellsworth participated in the framing, ratification, and implementation of the early American government, yet this founder has been very much forgotten. He is obscure, in part, because he was neither a partisan firebrand nor the leader of a powerful faction. He was a moderate, a conciliator, a principled man who often sought compromise. Nevertheless, as a forger of consensus he played a significant role in creating our union. His clout was not lost upon his peers. Aaron Burr commented ruefully that the influence of his Connecticut colleague over his fellow senators was so great that "if Ellsworth had happened to spell the name of the Deity with two d's, it would have taken the Senate three weeks to expunge the superfluous letter."[1] Indeed, few men of the founding generation mustered the intellectual courage to go toe-to-toe with James Madison in debate. At the Constitutional Convention, with the future plan of the U.S. government hanging in the balance, Ellsworth did just that. And he won.

Prior to the Constitutional Convention, Ellsworth was, in the phrase of the historians of the era, one of the "young men of the Revolution." Before turning thirty-five, Ellsworth was already a veteran of the Connecticut government as well as the Continental Congress. Returning to Philadelphia in the summer of 1787, Ellsworth emerged as a crucial actor in the camp that successfully argued for measured constitutional change. Following the Convention, supporters of the Constitution within Connecticut enlisted Ellsworth to present the case for the new plan of government to his state's ratification delegates. Connecticut ratified by a lopsided margin.

Throughout the 1790s, Ellsworth's involvement in all three branches of the federal government marked the apex of his political influence. During his service in the first Senate, Ellsworth drafted the historic legislation that created America's judicial system. In 1796, he became the chief justice of the United States. Only two men had held the post before Ellsworth. Four years later, John Adams turned to Ellsworth to carry out the "most decisive action" of Adams's presidency. He dispatched Ellsworth to France on a peace mission that many in Adams's own administration bitterly opposed.

While Ellsworth often managed to find compromise between competing political camps, unanimity was rarely the natural state of affairs in the early republic. In historian Thomas P. Slaughter's assessment,

> conflict was at the heart of the Revolution, and conflict among Americans was at least as important a part of the story as cooperation against a common enemy. In the aftermath of the violent international struggle that virtually ended in 1781, conflict remained the body and soul of American politics through the

end of the century. . . . Political change from 1780 through 1800—the victory of particular politicians, ideologies, and interests—was not understood by many participants as progressive, inevitable, or consistent with the principles of the Revolution.[2]

Against the backdrop of the genuine strife that characterized early American politics, Ellsworth's success in fashioning lasting political compromises, such as the Judiciary Act of 1789 (under which today's federal court system retains the same basic structure that Ellsworth designed for it two centuries ago), is all the more impressive.

This book is not a study of religious faith among the Founding Fathers. But it does raise one point about religion's role in the early American government. Whether most of the Founding Fathers were Christians or deists, Ellsworth was a devout Calvinist. His theological formation, moreover, was the source of his political pragmatism. For modern readers, Ellsworth's political pragmatism presents the following paradox. How was it that Ellsworth, who viewed politics largely through the lens of theology, was able to assert the moderate view while his more secular-minded colleagues frequently opted for more contentious policy agendas? Today, religion, often viewed as divisive, is considered an impediment to political compromise. Things were different at the founding. Amid the early debates over the role of the federal government, the future of slavery, and the conduct of foreign policy, to cite a few examples, it was Ellsworth's Calvinist faith that steered him—and often his colleagues with him—toward a lasting consensus.

Modern audiences may be accustomed to the marginalizing effect of theological beliefs on contemporary political leaders. Yet if holding deep-seated theological views makes a politician today unable to garner widespread support, Ellsworth's theological formation had much the opposite effect. Far from hampering his ability to shape the answers to the questions that vexed early American politicians, Ellsworth's theological convictions were often the very reason why he proved to be politically influential. His form of Calvinism provided a profound reason to seek broad compromises that protected the nation from external threats and internal strife. God's will, his particular creed told him, was to preserve America's harmony.

Beyond motivating his political pragmatism, Ellsworth's religious convictions also contributed to his enthusiasm for federalism. For some of America's founders, the division of power between the state and national governments was dangerously inefficient. For Ellsworth, by contrast, federalism was quasi-sacred. In his home state, towns formed independent political units, which, in turn, elected representatives to serve in Connecticut's General Assembly. Moreover, many of Connecticut's towns were originally organized around churches. Not only, then, was Connecticut's government a federal one, but its federalism had religious roots. None of this was lost upon Ellsworth, who, after three decades of service to the federal government, returned happily to his home in Windsor, where he would devote the final years of his life to, among other things, compiling a regular newspaper column on the latest agricultural techniques.

What follows, in short, is a study of a religious pragmatist, a devoted Federalist, who was responsible for making possible the lofty designs of better-known founders. Ellsworth's legacy, as we shall see, if not his name, endures.

CHAPTER ONE

THE EDUCATION OF A PURITAN POLITICIAN

Righteousness exalteth a nation.

—Reverend Joseph Bellamy, Election Sermon, 1762

"CONNECTICUT WAS A RELIGIOUS COMMUNITY"

Oliver Ellsworth was born on April 29, 1745, in a small British colony, "essentially isolated from the main currents and forces of the Anglo-American world," as one historian has put it.[1] Tucked into the backwater of North America, mid-eighteenth-century Connecticut consisted predominantly of middling farmers of English ancestry and Puritan religious convictions who raised large families and lived in remarkably homogeneous communities, none of which were much larger or smaller, richer or poorer, than the others.[2]

Founded in 1633 by Pilgrims from the Plymouth Colony in Massachusetts, Ellsworth's birthplace, sometimes called "Ancient Windsor," was Connecticut's first English settlement. Windsor soon became the domain of Englishmen from another colony also in present-day Massachusetts. By 1637, the initial settlers from

Plymouth sold most of their land in Windsor to émigrés from the Massachusetts Bay Colony. Other cadres from the Massachusetts Bay Colony laid claim to the Connecticut River Valley villages of Hartford and Wethersfield.[3]

In theology, the second wave of English settlers to Connecticut were Puritans, a descriptive that refers to the "broad fabric" of sixteenth- and seventeenth-century English Protestants who sought to reform the Church of England while remaining within the Anglican fold.[4] The Puritans who settled the Massachusetts Bay Colony and Connecticut were thus different from the Pilgrims who founded the Plymouth Colony. The latter included among their ranks separatist and semiseparatist dissenters, who sought to sever all ties with the Church of England, or were at least more inclined to favor such a break.

In many ways, the foundations laid by Connecticut's Puritan forefathers shaped the policies that Ellsworth supported during his various stints in federal office. Speaking of the Constitutional Convention, where Ellsworth would ably and successfully advance the interests of his home state, historian Forrest McDonald comments that the determining factor for the maneuvers of most of the delegates was "the interests and outlooks of the states and local areas they represented."[5] In particular, Connecticut's Puritan heritage established several pillars in the colony's political landscape, most importantly a preference for democratic elections of political leaders and orderly constitutional governance guided by the principle of federalism.

Among the reforms that they sought most, Puritans preferred that ministers be chosen by their congregations and not appointed by bishops, as was the practice in the Church of England.[6] Connecticut's early settlers considered the election of civil leaders also to be a moral duty. Soon after arriving in Connecticut, for example, Reverend Thomas Hooker (1583–1646), whose leadership of the "last and most famous" exodus of approximately one hundred Puritans from the Massachusetts Bay Colony to the village of Hartford has earned him the honorific title "the father of Connecticut," preached a famous sermon in which he contended that the formation of a civil government rested in "the free consent of the people," and that "the choice of public magistrates belongs unto the people, by God's own allowance."[7] The defense by Connecticut's Puritan founders of democratic elections for the colony's civil and religious leaders alike may be due to the fact that the distinction between secular and ecclesiastical governments was not nearly as widely drawn in pre-Revolutionary Connecticut as in present times. The colony's earliest settlers came largely as organized religious congregations, and the church buildings where they worshiped often served as the venue for the meetings of the town's elders, who were also, almost exclusively, respected members of the town church. "In the early years of the colony's existence," notes one historian, "an individual's chances of becoming either an admitted inhabitant or a freeman," referring, respectively, to those who could participate in town- and colony-wide affairs, "were nonexistent if he was not a member of the Congregational Church."[8] "From the beginning," remarks another, "Connecticut was a religious community."[9]

Connecticut's Puritan founders were responsible for setting in motion the colony's long history of orderly government. In 1639, representatives from Windsor, Hartford, and Wethersfield agreed to the Fundamental Orders. Because they were not ratified popularly and did not explicitly protect individual rights, the Fundamental Orders cannot be considered a constitution in the modern sense of the term. However, they did establish the rudimentary frame for Connecticut's first colonial government. And remarkably so. The drafters of the Orders had only a few years earlier arrived in Connecticut. Still, they managed in short order to establish a quasi-federal system of government that remained largely intact throughout the state's colonial history.

As for the federalist favor of the Fundamental Orders, the early plan of government recognized Connecticut's towns as the foundation of the colony's political life with authority over local matters. Issues that pertained to the "good of this comon welth," on the other hand, were to be handled by Connecticut's General Assembly.[10] There was most likely a religious imperative behind this division of power. Connecticut's earliest Puritan settlers were Congregationalists. In contrast with Presbyterians, who favored a more hierarchical church structure with some degree of coordination between individual congregations, Connecticut's Congregationalists preferred that their churches be led by their elected minister without much interference, if any, by other religious bodies.[11] One political manifestation of Connecticut's Congregationalism can be seen in the establishment of the colony's towns as distinct and equal units. Along with relegating the administration of local affairs to the towns, the Orders also set forth that the colony's towns would have an equal voice at the General Assembly, with each town entitled to send the same "three or four delegates" regardless of the town's population.[12]

In 1662, Great Britain formally granted Connecticut a royal charter, which became the colony's official governing document. The royal charter, however, only solidified the distribution of power already in effect under the Orders. Connecticut's towns remained the fundamental elements of the colony's political infrastructure.

These independent local units remained responsible for determining the state's electorate and sending thenceforth no more than two deputies to the colony's General Assembly, which directed the colony's general government.[13]

Connecticut's method of governing itself produced a remarkable degree of tranquility. Throughout the state's long colonial history, extended political strife was rare. Connecticut's electorate routinely reelected the same politicians. "Of the 111 men who served as governors, deputy governors, and members of the Council (the upper house of the Assembly)," tallies historian David M. Roth, "between the early 1660s and 1776, the average individual was elected and reelected fourteen times."[14]

While Connecticut used elections to fill the upper echelons of its colonial government, the colony's most important posts came to be held to a significant extent by members of a few families, the Pitkins, Allyns, Trumbulls, and Wolcotts among them. "The state of Connecticut has always been governed by an aristocracy," John Adams would later quip. "Half a dozen families, or at the most a dozen, have controlled that country when a colony, as well as since it has become a state."[15] While Connecticut was led by relatively few, the larger electorate was not completely excluded from the reins of government. Noah Webster, the compiler of the famous dictionary, remarked that Connecticut's political stability was a consequence of the colony's republican practice of holding annual elections for members of the state's lower house.[16]

Whatever the cause, Connecticut's politicians largely managed to retain the public's esteem, governing the state with due respect for the autonomy of the colony's various towns according to the protofederal principles that the Congregationalist-minded negotiators of the Fundamental Orders and the royal charter had long since established. On the centennial anniversary of the ratification of the royal charter, Reverend Joseph Bellamy, Ellsworth's preparatory-school tutor, neatly summarized the warm regard that Connecticut's inhabitants held for their colony's form of government:

> And as to civil privileges, no community under heaven enjoys greater than we do. Nor is it easy to conceive what greater civil privileges can be enjoyed than we enjoy. Once every year, we may unite as brethren, and choose out our wisest and ablest men, to make our laws, to guide our public affairs, and provide for the decision of all our civil controversies. And all our towns are so many corporations, invested with power to take care of their own public concerns, and suppress idleness and debauchery, and every kind of immorality. And even every little parish has, so far as it needs for its own well-being, as part of the whole, full power and authority to manage and order its own affairs. Meanwhile each family is a distinct kingdom of its own, and for the defense of its rights and properties stands entitled to the wisdom and strength of the whole community.[17]

ELLSWORTH'S LINEAGE

Ruled nearly from the beginning by steadfast Congregationalist farmers, "Ancient Windsor" would produce its fair share of colonial luminaries, a feat made more remarkable considering that Ellsworth's birthplace registered a population of only 2,302 in 1782.[18] A gravestone in the town's Old Burying Ground marks the resting place of Windsor-born Roger Wolcott (1679–1767), who spent more than three decades in Connecticut's colonial assembly before serving as governor from 1751–54. On the other side of the

Connecticut River, in East Windsor, Jonathan Edwards (1703–58), the future theological architect of the First Great Awakening, president of the College of New Jersey, and grandfather of Aaron Burr, was born.

Josiah Ellsworth, the great-grandfather of the Founding Father, was the first Ellsworth to migrate to Windsor from England—early Ellsworth biographers surmise that Josiah's roots lay in the northern county of Yorkshire. Although the reasons behind Josiah's decision to depart England remain a mystery, it is known that Josiah arrived in Windsor in 1654, almost two decades after the town's founding; that he subsequently purchased the family's home in North Windsor; and that he steadily acquired a position of good standing among his fellow townspeople. In 1657, Josiah was made a freeman, affording him the privilege of participating in the regular elections of his town's deputies to the colonial assembly.[19]

Few records remain of Jonathan Ellsworth, Josiah's sixth child and Oliver's grandfather, except that Jonathan was "a successful storekeeper and tavern-keeper." Jonathan's seventh child, David, Oliver's father, married Jemima Leavitt, with whom he had four children. Their eldest, also David, was born in 1742, followed by Oliver in 1745, Martin, who did not survive infancy, in 1750, and Oliver's younger sister Jemima in 1754.[20]

Though a dutiful father, David Ellsworth was notably absent at his son Oliver's birth. In April 1745, Captain Ellsworth was in command of a Windsor company of militiamen who had deployed with five hundred Connecticut soldiers under Major General Roger Wolcott, the future governor, as part of the British-led siege of the French fortress Louisburg on the St. Lawrence River in Canada. The successful forty-nine-day siege of Louisburg was a defining moment for the New England colonies. Remembered as "the pinnacle of colonial arms," the victory at Louisburg "convinced the colonists of the power of their amateur military system for a generation to come."[21]

After Louisburg, Oliver's father resumed his management of the family's farm. The familiar patterns of life in a largely self-contained colony returned. Without a commercial port or "an exportable product such as Massachusetts cod, Carolina rice, or Virginia tobacco," Connecticut maintained few commercial or cultural ties with Great Britain.[22] From what the secondary sources tell, David Ellsworth was one of the many plain Connecticut farmers whose universe was limited to the land upon which he toiled, the Congregationalist church where he worshiped, the town assembly hall where he gathered with his neighbors, and the home where he rested. But this circumscribed life seems not to have been perceived as a burden by Oliver's father. Most likely he passed on to his son the sincere appreciation that Oliver held for modest landholders and the simple townsfolk with whom Oliver happily mixed long after he retired from public life. The hard work and the frugality of Oliver's father, moreover, paid off in precisely the way that a pious New England farmer might have hoped it would. David accumulated a sizable, but not extravagant, estate and sufficient wealth to provide for his children without eliminating their need to labor for the betterment of their souls.[23]

Between Oliver's parents, it may have been his mother who had more influence over Oliver's upbringing. Jemima Ellsworth was remembered by a grandson as a "lady of excellent mind, good character, and pious principles."[24] In a superb recent Ellsworth biography, William R. Casto has unveiled new evidence of the depth of Jemima's piety. Casto notes that Ellsworth's father attended religious services at the Congregationalist First Society in Windsor until 1761, when the North Society was formed. Oliver's father had been among those who had petitioned the General Assembly to approve the formation of a Congregationalist parish that would be located north of the Rivulet (now the Farmington River) in response to the earlier creation of a separate meeting-house south of the Rivulet. Under the North Society's eventual rules, only parishioners who could show that they had a direct regenerating—or conversion—experience could receive communion. "Although Jemima Ellsworth," writes Casto, "was almost immediately admitted to the new church as a member in full communion, her husband, David, never was."[25]

"Justice for Nations"

It can be presumed that young Oliver had a quiet upbringing in which he attended school and performed his fair share of agrarian chores. Oliver would recall to a son that when he was raised, life in Windsor was difficult and the manners of the townspeople were simple. Windsor had only one carriage, and people ate from trenchers, the wooden tableware used by modest colonials in place of the pewter-made metal alternatives that wealthier contemporaries might have owned.[26]

One consequential fact, however, does separate Ellsworth's early upbringing from that of other American founders—Oliver's introduction to the political theology of the New Divinity Calvinists.

By the time Oliver was a boy, the Calvinist theology that he would receive from his eventual tutors had undergone a significant transformation due in no small part to events that occurred in the Connecticut River Valley. In 1740, George Whitefield convened a religious revival meeting in Windsor. Whitefield's visit to Windsor was part of his famous tour of the American colonies during which the English preacher captivated his listeners—the not ordinarily evangelical Benjamin Franklin among them—and spurred what historians have called the First Great Awakening, the mid-eighteenth-century Christian revival that reverberated throughout the colonies. Casto surmises that David and Jemima, recently married, attended the Windsor revival. A separate account indicates that the event was so well attended that the meetinghouse could not "accommodate the hundreds that came to hear the burning eloquence of the Man of God."[27]

Within Connecticut, Whitefield's preaching produced dissension as well. Connecticut's established clergy believed that Whitefield-style personal conversions threatened anarchy. Dismissing the revivalists as New Lights, and promoting themselves as Old Lights, Connecticut's established clergy persuaded the General Assembly to outlaw itinerant preaching. The ban, enacted in 1742, was crafted to limit the reach of New Light preachers, who, prior to the statute, had spread their message as itinerants, operating apart from any particular congregation, whose ministers were then typically Old Lights.[28]

When the turmoil between Old and New Lights first arose, the minister at the Windsor Congregationalist church where David and Jemima Ellsworth worshiped was into his fourth decade of ministry.[29] While esteemed by Old Lights as a respected ecclesiastical veteran, Reverend Joseph Marsh was also sympathetic to New Light theology. Five years before Whitefield's tour, Marsh's church had experienced a protoawakening at which there was a "remarkable pouring out of the Spirit of God" and "a great ingathering of souls to Christ," and during which Marsh, later praised by

Whitefield as a "truly converted man," himself had a regenerating experience.[30]

As further evidence of their theological leanings, it is noteworthy that the Ellsworths sent Oliver to study under Joseph Bellamy, the colony's leading New Light minister. While it is unclear when exactly Oliver began his tutelage under Reverend Bellamy, it may be estimated that Oliver was around twelve years old. In 1762, at the age of seventeen, Ellsworth completed his studies under Reverend Bellamy and began his undergraduate coursework at Yale College.[31]

The significance of the perhaps five years that Ellsworth spent studying under Bellamy—"a forceful, demanding, and dominating teacher," by biographer Casto's estimation—is that Bellamy supplied Ellsworth with the prime motivation behind the Connecticut leader's lifelong political pragmatism. The tenets of New Divinity Calvinism offered a theological justification for governing through incremental steps, reserving bolder maneuvers for when a majority of the polity supported sanctioning an isolated crop of dissenters.[32]

In a tract entitled *Four Sermons on the Wisdom of God in the Permission of Sin*, Bellamy set forth the principles of New Divinity Calvinism. Ellsworth would reference *Wisdom of God* on more than one occasion during his public career, evidencing the Connecticut politician's familiarity with the tract.[33] Given that *Wisdom of God* was published in 1758, roughly when Ellsworth began his tutelage under Bellamy, it is likely that Ellsworth was quickly introduced to the tract's central themes.

In *Wisdom of God*, Bellamy advised his audiences to concern themselves primarily with the overarching, divine scheme for the universe. Phrases such as "the whole moral system," "his grand and glorious scheme," "the wisdom of the whole," "God's grand plan," the "general good of the moral system," the "glorious designs and noble ends which infinite wisdom has in view," "his universal plan," and "the whole intelligent system" appear throughout the text.[34] For Bellamy, recognizing and living according to the large theological picture was the faithful Christian's essential task. "Our highest moral rectitude, perfection, and happiness," he emphasized, "must arise from, and consist in an enlarged, clear, lively view of God and ourselves."

What Bellamy discovered, furthermore, when he looked at the revealed history of divine intervention in human affairs was that God was not a governor inclined to rash judgments, imprudent overreaching, or immoderate commands. Rather, God acted patiently and incrementally so that from "small beginnings" faithful followers could "grow up to a more full knowledge of God, and insight into his moral government of the world."[35] God treated humanity, claimed Bellamy, with the wisdom of an intelligent lawmaker who crafts the law in such a way that the people ultimately support and ratify it with their free and willing consent, reforming themselves rather than rejecting the sovereign's wishes. God let the people of Israel wander for forty years in the desert, Bellamy explained in a characteristic example, because "nothing impresses the heart of a human creature like facts. Nor could any series of facts have been better contrived than these to reach their hearts."[36]

With respect to politics, Bellamy advised that the correct approach was not to forsake the world, but to strive to improve it through prudent governance. "Wisdom consists in choosing the best end," he remarked, "and contriving the most proper means to attain it."[37] Bellamy advocated that earthly powers mimic God's divine restraint. Rather than hastily condemning those who acted immorally, Bellamy recommended, political leaders ought to wait patiently, building up their case so that the offending party ultimately sees the error of his or her misconduct. "In some cases," advised Bellamy, "even we ourselves have a *right*, in a sense, to permit sin, and may act wisely in doing so, as common sense teaches all mankind." He described a scenario in which a "wise and good master, who has a very lazy, unfaithful, deceitful servant," craftily decides to "let [the servant] take his course, with a view more thoroughly to convict him, and reform him," adding that the master's chosen course of action did not amount to "*doing evil that good may come*, but acting wisely, in order to reclaim a lazy, deceitful servant."[38] Convinced of the reality of original sin, Bellamy believed that making men moral was no easy task. From his perspective, the solution was neither to withdraw from the world nor to surrender to it. In recommending a restrained approach to correcting human failings, New Divinity Calvinism offered adherents such as Ellsworth "a powerful justification for political compromise."[39]

Along with the hardheaded pragmatism that Ellsworth exhibited at various moments during his career in public office, independent evidence supports the conclusion that Ellsworth's approach to politics was informed by New Divinity theological principles. After retiring from national office, Ellsworth collaborated in the authoring of *A Summary of Christian Doctrine and Practice*. The religious tract, which Ellsworth coauthored with members of the Connecticut Missionary Society, reiterated the central points that Bellamy had made roughly a half century earlier. Along with his collaborators, Ellsworth asserted that since "sinless obedience" was unattainable, Christians were obliged instead to maintain a "general walk with God." In keeping with New Divinity theology, *A*

Summary of Christian Doctrine stated that "external action is not, by itself, either holy or sinful," but that sin involved the "temper of the heart." The emphasis on the intentions of the actor, rather than on the conduct itself, was a necessary corollary of the New Divinity principle that prudent Christian rulers could tolerate evil as long as they had the right intention of bringing the citizenry closer to fulfilling the divine plan for human happiness.[40]

Another aspect of Bellamy's theology that shaped Ellsworth's thought, leading the future Connecticut politician to favor policies that punished dissident political minorities within the emerging republic, was the influential minister's notion that God did not simply judge individuals but was also keenly interested in the conduct of entire communities—and, moreover, would not necessarily wait until the hereafter before showing His mercy or wrath upon the various nations. "Righteousness exalteth a nation, as it is in itself an honorable thing; as it has a natural tendency to make a nation prosperous and happy," Bellamy explained in the 1762 sermon that he delivered to the Connecticut General Assembly on the centennial of the colony's royal charter.[41] Yet if God blessed entire nations for their virtue, the same divine sovereign, warned Bellamy, also punished whole polities for the vices of their members. "Our own vices may render us very miserable," Bellamy continued. "For notwithstanding the goodness of our land, and all our advantages for navigation, yet luxury, idleness, debauchery, dishonesty, and multiplied lawsuits, may bring us to poverty."[42]

To be sure, the notion that God intervenes in human affairs to render His judgments upon whole communities was not a Puritan novelty. In the New Testament, Paul of Tarsus taught that Christians were members of one body and thus affected by the health of the other parts. "If one part is suffering," wrote Paul, "all the rest suffer with it; if one part is treated with honor, all the rest find pleasure in it" (1 Corinthians 12:26). What was new in Puritanism—and what would critically influence Oliver Ellsworth, among others shaped by Puritan thought—was, precisely, the locus of the corporate accountability. While maintaining the concept of corporate accountability, Puritans concentrated it on individual congregations. And since Puritan congregations also exercised considerable political authority, it would soon become routine for Puritans to transfer the notion of common destiny from the congregation to the polity. Thus, John Winthrop would famously instruct the first settlers of the Massachusetts Bay Colony,

> The eyes of all people are upon us. So that if we shall deal falsely with our God in this work we have undertaken, and so cause Him to withdraw His present help from us, we shall be made a story and a by-word through the world. We shall open the mouths of enemies to speak evil of the ways of God, and all professors for God's sake. We shall shame the faces of many of God's worthy servants, and cause their prayers to be turned into curses upon us till we be consumed out of the good land whither we are going.[43]

Following in the tradition of Winthrop, Ellsworth's tutor, Reverend Bellamy, would likewise apply the concept of divine accountability to a secular polity (albeit, as in the case of the Massachusetts Bay Colony, a polity that had a Puritan foundation and continued to elect righteous rulers): "And while our idleness, our extravagances, our parties, our errors, and our wickedness in general, all join to render us a miserable people," Bellamy reminded the citizens of Connecticut, "they will at the same time naturally prepare us for, and bring down, the judgments of God upon us."[44]

The effect of the transfer of the notion of divine retribution from the Christian faithful universal to individual congregations and finally to secular entities was to give political leaders a strong impetus for ensuring that the citizenry avoided moral failings that were sufficiently depraved as to compel God's wrath on the whole body politic. It also encouraged righteous leaders to consider harsh actions against isolated members of the whole community who acted contrary to God's will, and who thus threatened to bring down God's judgment, once again, against the entire polity. Significantly, Bellamy viewed harmonious existence between different groups of citizens as a signal that the citizenry was acting righteously. For this reason, he exalted the general tolerance that then existed among Connecticut's Congregationalists, Baptists, Presbyterians, and Anglicans, while deploring lawsuits and denominational conflict.[45] But by associating righteousness with civic harmony, Bellamy elevated political consensus as an outcome to be desired by moral leaders.

In Ellsworth's case, the overall consequence of the Puritan and later New Divinity focus on the divine accountability of secular polities and the related importance of civil harmony most likely had the effect of counterbalancing the Connecticut politician's ideological preference for local self-determination. His New Divinity background rounded out his outlook such that Ellsworth was able to support a constitutional balance that recognized the autonomy of the states along with the need for an effective national government and a genuine national identity. Ellsworth's theological convictions led him to the belief that God would hold the whole political community responsible for the sins of a few. Echoing Winthrop and Bellamy, Ellsworth would write in a 1788 defense of the Constitution, "The Creator of nature and its laws made justice as necessary for nations as for individuals, and this necessity hath been sealed by the fate of all obstinate offenders. If you will not hear your own groans, nor feel the pangs of your own torture, it must continue until removed by a political annihilation. Such as do not pity themselves cannot be long be pitied."[46]

Once the separate American colonies began to act as a unified nation, as would be the case during the Revolutionary War, Ellsworth would apply to the young nation the concept of corporate accountability and, accordingly, favor national solutions to prevent an adverse divine judgment, particularly in cases where a minority of states stood against the consensus of the nation. America "could not violate her faith," Ellsworth would write at a time when the Continental Congress was considering measures that would weaken the value of the nation's early currency, "without incensing the Almighty and daring his vengeance against her."[47] A decade later, Ellsworth began his opening speech in favor of the Constitution at Connecticut's ratification convention by comparing the states under the existing Articles of Confederation to "the Canaanitish nations" of the Old Testament, "whose divided situation rendered them an easy prey."[48] While serving as U.S. chief justice, Ellsworth emphasized that "national laws [under the Constitution] are that means by which it pleases heaven to make of weak and discordant parts, one great people."[49] Finally, in *A Summary of Christian Doctrine*, Ellsworth further emphasized the moral value of political unity. "The Bible," the former chief justice and his fellow authors explained, authorized public officers to do "whatever is essential to the common weal." Righteous rulers were to prefer "the true interest of the state to any partial interest" and to devote themselves to "protecting all in their rights and guarding the common interest."[50]

Underlying Ellsworth's support for a national government, then, was a theme suffusing the Connecticut lawyer's years of religious instruction and study. Reverend Bellamy had taught young Oliver that the purpose of life was to determine the grand divine plan that God had for the world and to ensure that it came to pass. God's plan for America, from Ellsworth's perspective, was that it be a single nation made of individual parts. At critical moments in the formation of the young republic, Ellsworth displayed his willingness to make the hard decisions that he deemed necessary for America to unite as a federal republic. It was God's plan for America to join as such, after all.

CHAPTER TWO

REVOLUTIONARY LESSONS

It is better to hazard something than to hazard all.

—Oliver Ellsworth, July 11, 1783

COLLEGIATE HARMONY

At the age of seventeen, in the autumn of 1762, Oliver Ellsworth concluded his tutelage under Bellamy and entered Yale College. Established sixty-one years earlier by the British merchant Elihu Yale, the college was then the central training grounds for Connecticut's Congregationalist clergy. Yale's founder had insisted that every student "shall consider the main end of his study to wit to know God in Jesus Christ and answerably to lead a Godly sober life." Connecticut's sole college was also the alma mater of Jonathan Edwards and Bellamy.[1]

Oliver's stay in New Haven, however, would be brief. At the time, the Christian harmony exalted by New Divinity theology was absent from Yale. The year before Ellsworth's enrollment, relations between the students and Yale's strict president, Thomas Clap, devolved to the point at which several students attacked a university tutor with clubs, then broke all the tutors' and President Clap's windows with pistol fire.[2]

Ellsworth soon found himself the subject of disciplinary action. During his first year at Yale, the administration cited Ellsworth for cleaning the college yard, which had recently become an offense when students had begun using the guise of tidying up the college yard to organize demonstrations against Yale.[3] The following year, Ellsworth was reprimanded again, this time for the consumption of "general treat or compotation of wine." In the estimation of one biographer, "these performances do not strike one as very damning. They do, however, seem to prove that Ellsworth was once a boy, and that the boys of colonial New England were not entirely unlike their descendants—at least when they went to college."[4]

Yale eventually forgave Ellsworth's youthful indiscretions, conferring an honorary degree upon the Connecticut politician. But this consolation would come three decades later. In the immediate wake of the drinking incident, Oliver left Yale at the request of his parents. His next stop was Princeton.

Originally chartered as the College of New Jersey, Princeton was founded in 1746, just one year after Ellsworth's birth. In contrast with Yale, Princeton displayed signs of the harmony championed by Ellsworth's New Divinity tutor. Established in New Jersey, a middle colony, Princeton attracted students from throughout the colonies. Whereas more than 90 percent of Yale's students were New Englanders, no single region so dominated Princeton. Sixty percent of the young college's students came from New York, New Jersey, and Pennsylvania; New England and the southern colonies contributed 28 and 12 percent, respectively, of the student population.[5] The geographical diversity of Princeton's students provided Ellsworth what may be considered his first "nationalizing" experience.

Founded in part as a religious institution to train New Light ministers, Princeton promoted religious liberty for Protestants. The same religious comity that Bellamy praised in his 1762 election sermon as existing between various Protestant denominations within Connecticut was sought by Bellamy's friend, Samuel Finley, who was Princeton's president. During Ellsworth's first year at Princeton, Finley wrote, "To inculcate or even recommend the discriminating opinions" within the college "of any one protestant denomination in preference to another, is carefully avoided."[6]

When Oliver arrived at Princeton, the college's academic life revolved around the university's debating societies, one of which—the Well Meaning Club—Ellsworth would help establish. Notably, no colonial college would train as many future speakers on the floor of the Continental Congress and the Constitutional Convention as Ellsworth's alma mater. The geographical mix of Princeton students, combined with the propensity of the debating societies to weigh in on matters of national interest, such as the imposition of the Stamp Act, make the academic scene at Princeton in the 1760s appear almost as a preview of the various continental assemblies that lay in the near future. Ellsworth's small graduating class included Luther Martin, a New Jerseyan who would later take up residence in Maryland and with whom Ellsworth would lock horns at the Constitutional Convention. Ellsworth likely also became acquainted with William Paterson, who continued to reside at Princeton despite graduating from the college the year prior to Ellsworth's arrival. Paterson and Ellsworth would work closely together as coauthors of the Judiciary Act of 1789. James Madison, Aaron Burr, Benjamin Rush, and Henry Lee are a few of the other early national leaders who attended Princeton around the same time as Ellsworth.[7]

One of the few corroborated episodes during Oliver's time at Princeton displays the emergence of the young student's persuasive talents. Before completing his degree, Oliver once more found himself the subject of official sanction, this time for violating the school's prohibition against wearing a hat in the college yard. Ellsworth protested that a hat must consist of a crown and brim. Because he had torn off the brim, Ellsworth contended that his headpiece lacked an element essential to all hats, and thus he could not be punished. Whether by force of the student's logic or of his self-confidence, the administration relented.[8]

Upon graduating from Princeton in 1766, Ellsworth returned to Connecticut, where he studied theology under Reverend John Smalley, a Congregationalist minister who had also studied under Bellamy at Yale. It soon became apparent, however, that Ellsworth's interests lay outside the realm of theology. When Smalley asked his young student to prepare a sermon, Ellsworth produced a draft that better resembled a legal argument. The former collegiate debater had spent the first ten pages of his proposed sermon carefully defining the terms that he intended to use. After reviewing Ellsworth's effort, Smalley granted him permanent leave to pursue another calling.[9]

Oliver's unwillingness to become a Congregationalist minister did not signal a rejection of the Congregationalist faith. For the entirety of his life Ellsworth was a regular churchgoer who prayed daily and invoked his faith with his children. "This life is but an embryo of our existence," he wrote his daughter Abigail in December 1791, "and derives its consequences only from its connection with future scenes."[10]

The tenets of New Divinity Calvinism would remain a critical part of Ellsworth's political outlook. As he explained to Count de Volney after the philosopher shared his plans for restructuring the

French government, "there is one thing for which you have made no provision—the selfishness of man."[11] Throughout his career in national office, we shall see, Ellsworth would seek to bring harmony to the new republic not through idealistic philosophical designs or far-reaching public policies, but by political prudence.

Legal Apprenticeship

Released from his postcollegiate training for the ministry, Oliver decided immediately to become a lawyer. During the colonial period, the common practice for aspiring lawyers was to apprentice—at some expense to the attorney in training—under an established practitioner. Ellsworth chose to associate first with Matthew Griswold, a prominent Connecticut lawyer, before switching to Jesse Root, a younger and likely less expensive alternative.[12]

Ellsworth was compelled to go into debt in order to meet the fees that he was required to pay the two attorneys, which implies that his father may have declined to support his son's career change. But if Ellsworth's father refused to underwrite his son's entry to the bar, ties between father and son remained. When Oliver married in 1772, David leased his son a small farm in Wintonbury (now Bloomfield), then a small village outside Hartford.[13]

In 1771, four years after beginning his apprenticeship, Oliver was admitted to the Connecticut bar. For young attorneys in Connecticut, the path to success was long. This was true also for Ellsworth. His fees totaled a single pound in his first year of practice; he supplemented his income by selling the timber that he axed on a parcel of woodland that he owned.[14]

The modest start to Ellsworth's professional career further cultivated his penchant for practicality. Oliver kept his law office in Hartford but lived on his family's small farm in Wintonbury, most likely because he could not afford another residence. Unable to purchase a carriage, Oliver covered on foot the five-mile distance, each way, between Wintonbury and Hartford. During one journey, a wealthier citizen commuting by carriage stopped Oliver and commented that walking to work was beneath an attorney. Undeterred, Ellsworth took the correction in stride—literally. He promptly replied that everyone had to spend some time of his or her life walking, and that he preferred to fulfill his quota while he was still young and fit.[15]

Marriage and Harmony

In 1772, a year after entering the bar, Oliver married Abigail Wolcott. Abigail was sixteen when the couple married. According to local lore, Oliver, who was just shy of eleven years older than Abigail, was initially taken with Abigail's elder sister. But while paying her a visit, Oliver was immediately smitten by Abigail's elegant demeanor and striking black eyes. Ellsworth himself was physically impressive. He stood over six feet tall, possessed a robust build, and carried himself with an unadorned dignity that was common among the pious gentlemen of eighteenth-century Connecticut. His strong jaw gave an appearance of sternness, particularly when he was a young man.[16]

Abigail happened to be related to the late Roger Wolcott, the long-serving Connecticut governor. The marriage between a then unknown attorney and the daughter of one of Connecticut's most prominent and well-connected families demonstrates the egalitarianism that lay at the heart of the colony's culture. Residents of Connecticut judged each other according to their personal industry, thrift, sobriety, honesty, and good character. By all these counts, Oliver was a worthy candidate for the hand of Abigail.

Oliver remained forever devoted to Abigail. They would have nine children, seven of whom survived infancy. When political duties demanded Oliver's absence from his home, he corresponded with Abigail dutifully and tenderly. In the midst of the Constitutional Convention, Oliver paused to inform Abigail that to stay healthy he had taken to walking "a good deal in the cool of the afternoons" and making frequent stops to "take in a little chat and tea sipping with good Connecticut women" who were residing in Philadelphia. When called away for historic gatherings, such as the Constitutional Convention, Oliver reassured Abigail that he remained attached to his home. During his sojourn to Philadelphia for the great Convention, he wrote Abigail, "This city has no charms for me. I mix with company without enjoying it and am perfectly tired with flattery and forms. To be very fashionable we must be very trifling and make and receive a thousand professions which everyone knows there is no truth in. Give me a little domestic circle where affection is natural and friendship sincere and I do not care who takes the rest."[17]

Oliver's letters to Abigail were formal, in keeping with the standard of the time. He would share with Abigail the latest political news, but, all the while, Oliver's genuine fondness for his wife was never far from his thoughts. "Should I hear, as I hope I shall that you & the little ones are all well," he began one letter to Abigail, "it will add greatly to the joy I feel in common with others on the arrival of Peace," referring to the end of the Revolutionary War.[18] "Dear Mrs. Ellsworth," Oliver addressed Abigail shortly after arriving in New York for the inauguration of the new Congress in 1789: "You will be glad to hear that I arrived safely in three days from Hartford, and that I am accommodated with lodgings in a good family." The newly elected senator proceeded to inform Abigail about the expected inauguration of President Washington and Vice President Adams (the Electoral College's results not being final). Following a concise report from the fledgling national capital, Oliver returned to what was in his heart. "That your life and health and that of the dear children may be preserved you'll readily believe is the daily petition of an affectionate friend," he closed the dispatch.[19]

Abigail's devotion to Oliver was also complete. Oliver's income remained paltry after their marriage, which compelled Abigail to tackle a share of the work on the couple's small farm. On a memorable occasion, Abigail managed to tend to an infant while milking the family cow by attaching a string to the cradle, enabling her to rock the baby as she continued the chore.[20] During the course of Oliver's public life, Abigail gracefully played hostess to several of the nation's leading public figures. On his tour of New England, which he undertook shortly after his first election, President Washington left a diary entry that records a stop at the Ellsworths' home: "Oct. 21st, 1789, by promise, I was to have breakfasted with Mr. Ellsworth in Windsor on my way to Springfield, but the morning proved very wet, and the rain not ceasing until ten o'clock, I did not set out till half after that hour. I called however and stayed an hour."[21] During his administration's diplomatic impasse with France, President Adams, too, made a visit to the Ellsworths' home. The president and Ellsworth, then U.S. chief justice, visited for two hours.[22] Guests no doubt observed that Abigail kept the family's home much the same way that Oliver carried himself in public, with refined simplicity. Wherever the exigencies of public service brought Oliver, he was never conflicted about where he wished to be—at the "pleasantest place" that he knew, home in Windsor with Abigail.[23]

Together with Abigail, Oliver saw that his children were attentively taught. His two youngest—twin boys—would follow him into public life. William Wolcott Ellsworth became a congressman, governor of Connecticut, and judge on the state's Supreme Court. Following the enactment of the Indian Removal Act, President Andrew Jackson appointed Henry Ellsworth to serve as Commissioner of Indian Tribes in Arkansas and Oklahoma. Jackson later made Henry the first commissioner of the United States Patent Office. Oliver Jr., Ellsworth's eldest son to survive infancy, accompanied his father to France on his namesake's final act of service to the nascent national government. Young Oliver's death in 1805 weighed heavily on the elder statesman during the final two years of his own life.[24]

Oliver's correspondence shows the intimacy that he shared with his children. "Dear Nabby," the senator began one missive to his daughter Abigail, using the nickname he had given her. "Your welcome letter of the 7th of this month reached me a few days since. I am exceedingly glad to hear that the family are all well, and in particular your mamma and the two little ones," referring to the recently arrived twins, William and Henry. "Your idea that they will make two fine men is very pleasing to me and I devotedly wish it may be realized." Ellsworth proceeded to express his sorrow over "the loss of the persons who have died in Windsor since I left it, and especially of Perry Newberry." The senator's humility did not end there. "[Miss Wadsworth] has some advantages beyond what you had—a richer and more fashionable father," he joked before closing the missive with some characteristic fatherly advice: "If you find any leisure, which will probably be very little, I wish you would amuse yourself with books. It is mental improvement after all which alone can give sweetness to manners and durability to charms."[25]

During the diplomatic mission that he would make to France a decade later, Ellsworth paused on several occasions to write to his children. "Daddy is a great way off," he began one letter to his twin sons, whom he nicknamed "Billy and Harry," "but he thinks about his little boys every day; and he hopes they are very good boys and learn their books well and say their prayers every night, and then God will love them as much as daddy does." Later in the same letter, Oliver told his sons how he narrowly escaped a dangerous attack, but he consoled them by promising that he was taking the necessary precautions to ensure a safe return. "The robbers," wrote Ellsworth, "came around the house where daddy lives the other night and the gardener shot off his two-barrel gun and killed two of them; and daddy believes if the robbers come into his room they will get killed, for he keeps a gun and two pistols charged all the times; and when he comes home he intends to give his gun to Martin and his pistols to Billy and Harry."[26]

To his death, Oliver would remain a devoted spouse and father.[27]

PROFESSIONAL SUCCESS

At the time that Ellsworth began practicing law, Connecticut's General Assembly appointed the colony's judiciary. As a result, an assemblyman who was also a practicing attorney could bring a case before a judge whose tenure depended on the assemblyman's vote in the legislature. Since many litigants sought to take advantage of the leverage that lawyers doubling as lawmakers had over the colony's judges, a lawyer-assemblyman could expect a profitable practice.

In 1773, at the age of twenty-eight, Ellsworth followed a path well-trod by attorneys before him by winning a seat to represent Windsor in the General Assembly. Following his reelection in the spring of 1774, Ellsworth obtained his first appointed post when his colleagues made him justice of the peace for Hartford County. In Connecticut's colonial government, the justice of the peace was responsible for deciding both civil and criminal matters where the damages fell below a certain threshold. Though Ellsworth was not yet thirty years old, the appointment hardly signaled his arrival in the innermost corridors of influence: he was just one of seventy justices of the peace appointed in Connecticut that year.[28]

During the summer of 1774, Oliver and Abigail celebrated the birth of their first child, Abigail. Shortly thereafter, the family left the small farm that Oliver had leased from his father and purchased a six-acre lot in Hartford. The move ended Oliver's chances of returning to the General Assembly as a delegate from his hometown, indicating that he esteemed his career as an attorney over security in the legislature.[29]

After several years of private practice, Ellsworth "no longer went to court with an empty docket." Indeed, his early success at the bar had quickly made him one of Connecticut's most sought-after litigators. While serving as his apprentice in 1779, Noah Webster tallied the number of cases on Ellsworth's docket as reaching as many as fifteen hundred. No other litigator in Connecticut was busier.[30]

Although Ellsworth's move to Hartford signaled an early retirement from public office—at least temporarily—events outside Connecticut would suddenly rearrange political priorities throughout the colonies.

"A Beautiful and Respectable Government"

On April 19, 1775, fighting between American militiamen and British soldiers erupted in the Massachusetts towns of Lexington and Concord. In Connecticut, public opinion of the era's most crucial political question was settled. Over the previous decade, the colony's ascendant politicians—including the young attorney Oliver Ellsworth—had sought to protect Connecticut from British interference.

No record of Ellsworth's views on independence exists for the momentous period when Connecticut threw in its lot with the rest of the American states and severed ties with Great Britain. But it is clear that this son of a captain who had fought for the British Crown harbored no reservations about the Revolution. His support for independence can be inferred from his place in the mainstream of Connecticut's political culture at the time of independence.

From the adoption of the Fundamental Orders in 1639, Connecticut had governed itself as a semi-independent republic. Connecticut's first constitution placed the British government—Crown or Parliament—nowhere in the frame of government that it established for the new colony. The 1662 royal charter that Connecticut later received from Great Britain only solidified the political arrangement in effect since the adoption of the Fundamental Orders, which had left Connecticut under the supervision of officeholders whom Connecticut's eligible voters themselves elected. Under the royal charter, the colony's electorate retained the privilege of electing deputies to the colony's General Assembly. The royal charter also maintained the largely unsupervised powers that Connecticut's colonial legislature had wielded since the adoption of the Fundamental Orders. Connecticut was not required by the royal charter to submit its assembly's proposed acts to the British government for final approval. Nor did the charter create a royal governor appointed by Great Britain. The charters of most of the other American colonies mandated a greater degree of formal oversight. "Connecticut was indeed a fortunate colony," summarizes one historian. "It practiced a fuller measure of self-government than did any other British province excepting Rhode Island."[31]

Beginning in the 1760s, Britain's attempt to exert greater control over the American colonies chilled relations between the virtually independent residents of Connecticut and the government of the mother country. The Stamp Act (1765) met immediate opposition in Connecticut. The colony's stamp distributor was seized by a band of five hundred men, who forced him to read the letter of resignation that they had prepared for him within hearing distance of the Connecticut assembly. The colonial lawmakers responded to the protest before them by agreeing to dispatch delegates to the Stamp Act Congress, thus adding Connecticut's voice to the intercolonial outcry over Parliament's recent act. The following spring, Connecticut's electorate voiced its support for a strong posture against perceived British overreaching. The colony's governor, who had sought to accommodate Great Britain, and four lawmakers were replaced with a ticket hand-selected by Connecticut's Stamp Act opponents.[32]

Perhaps due to Connecticut's history of self-government, there was considerable sentiment in favor of independence. Asked by Virginia patriot Patrick Henry at a session of the first Continental Congress in 1774 why his fellow residents of Connecticut stood more firmly for "the cause of liberty than the people of other states," Roger Sherman, alongside whom Ellsworth would serve at the Constitutional Convention, reportedly replied, "Because we have more to lose than any of them."[33] The pride that Connecticut's residents had in their political independence from any superintending worldly power had been well established. "This is a beautiful and respectable Government," Reverend Joseph Fish remarked in a characteristic tribute. "Liberty stretches from her and without Control, to give her Suffrages for Men to rule . . . in the Fear of God."[34]

Following Lexington and Concord in 1775, proindependence forces in the General Assembly showed their strength. Without delay or opposition, the General Assembly stood up a reserve force and outfitted two sloops. General Washington would praise Connecticut's energetic response to the outbreak of war. In a sign that revealed, separately, the extent to which the practical-minded leaders of Connecticut's wartime government deemed allegiance to the cause of independence of higher value than protecting political speech, the General Assembly made it an offense punishable by jail to defame the acts of Congress or the colony's legislature. For their part, the citizens of Connecticut also supported the state's mobilization efforts. By the summer of 1776, Connecticut had stood up nearly nineteen thousand troops from within its borders, which amounted to as much as 45 percent of the state's adult male population responding to the call to arms.[35]

Because Connecticut had few loyalists compared with most of the states and a government that had been functionally autonomous since the previous century, independence did little to alter the colony's political architecture. In 1776, Connecticut's General Assembly agreed that "the ancient form of civil government contained" in its existing charter "shall be and remain the civil constitution of this state, under the sole authority of the people hereof, independent of any king or prince whatsoever." By a vote of Connecticut's legislature, the state was now independent of the British Crown. But the form of government was the same. Throughout the Revolutionary era, independent Connecticut remained governed largely by the deputies that the towns selected to serve in the state's powerful legislature.[36]

"The Darkest Hour"

While independence did not alter Connecticut's form of government, it had a great effect on Ellsworth's career. Had not the fighting in Massachusetts occurred when it did, Ellsworth may have had to wait some time to join the effort. Notified that fighting had erupted in Massachusetts, Governor Jonathan Trumbull convened an emergency session of the Connecticut legislature on April 26, 1775. By now relocated to Hartford, Ellsworth had only fifteen days remaining in his tenure as a deputy from Windsor when Trumbull called upon the deputies. At the ensuing emergency session, Ellsworth obtained a position on the newly created Committee of the Pay Table, which oversaw Connecticut's spending on the war with Britain.

Ellsworth's position put him in line for a pair of important assignments that followed from the committee's work. In February 1776, Connecticut's Council of Safety, a quasi–war department, requested that an official from the pay table travel to Cambridge, Massachusetts, where General Washington was camped with the Continental Army. The selected committee member was ordered to petition the commander in chief for $100,000, the sum needed to reimburse Connecticut for the military expenses the colony had incurred since Lexington and Concord. The committee nominated Ellsworth. The young civilian would have his first audience with America's most revered officer—although Ellsworth would have to approach Washington as a supplicant, tasked with asking the commander in chief in person for a refund of Connecticut's war debts. The general agreed to forward Ellsworth's request to the Continental Congress. Ellsworth left no account of his initial meeting with Washington, who two decades later would turn to then Senator Ellsworth to fill the vacant seat of chief justice on the U.S. Supreme Court.

Returning to Connecticut, Ellsworth briefed the colony's war council on his meeting and nominated himself to follow up on the action. The council members resolved that Ellsworth or another official should "repair to the Continental Congress and apply for repayment of said sums." In the end, two members of Connecticut's congressional delegation, already in Philadelphia, handled the assignment, depriving Ellsworth of the opportunity to present Connecticut's case before the national assembly. But Ellsworth had gained the trust of his state's authorities. In May 1776, the General Assembly nominated Ellsworth for his second fundraising mission. This time Ellsworth was dispatched to Major General Philip Schuyler's camp in Albany to seek reimbursement from Schuyler, the commander of the Continental Army's Canadian campaign, for the sums that Connecticut had paid its troops serving under Schuyler's command.[37]

As the war continued, so did the dividends of Ellsworth's position on the pay table. The post put him in contact with local as well as statewide elites. In December 1776, the Connecticut General Assembly dispatched Ellsworth and eighteen others to the western part of the state to drum up enlistments in the colony's militia. According to one biographer, Ellsworth's acceptance of this assignment was "an overt display" of his support for the struggle for independence. Western Connecticut had been the center of gravity for Connecticut's loyalist opposition. Fortunately for Ellsworth, the recruiting effort apparently did not generate any violent exchanges with Tory partisans. In October 1777, the legislature nominated the thirty-two-year-old Ellsworth as one of the state's seven delegates to represent Connecticut at the Continental Congress.[38]

A tragic personal loss delayed Ellsworth's entry into congressional service. In October 1776, Abigail had given birth to the couple's second child, a son named Oliver Ellsworth Jr. The arrival of Ellsworth's namesake coincided with the family's relocation to an impressive residence in Hartford which Oliver had purchased, having established himself in the city. In May 1778, Oliver Jr. fell ill and died in the family's home. "This world has now fewer charms in my eyes than it once had & I have no doubt but you can say the same," wrote a devastated Ellsworth to Abigail one year after their son's death. "Happy for us," Oliver continued in the same letter, "if it keeps a better world more constantly in view, and is a means of bringing us to those joys and rest into which I fully believe our dear departed little son is already entered."[39]

Stricken by the loss of his son, Oliver did not take up a seat in Congress until the fall of 1778. Although Ellsworth had been nominated as a congressional delegate a year earlier, this was the first time he stepped inside the halls of the federal capitol. The earliest record that Ellsworth left behind from his congressional service was a letter to his wife Abigail dated January 9, 1779. "Dear Girl," he began. "Was you to see me this night, in the situation I am, with a beard a week old, with the cape of my great Coat buttoned about my ears, and a large muffler of Baize across my nose and mouth, I am sure you would not give me a kiss." Ellsworth later described how he had spent Christmas two weeks earlier. The new city brought a new experience to the Connecticut attorney in the form of Catholic worship. "I went among the papists and attended divine service in a romish chapel," he wrote, "where I confess I was wonderfully struck with the shows of the place, the superstition of the ceremonies and devotion of the people."[40]

Over the next several years, Ellsworth would dispatch frequent reports to his state's governor, signed jointly by his fellow delegates from Connecticut. These letters detailed official business. But they too had their share of zeal. Ellsworth had the fate of joining Congress for what one historian called "the darkest hour of the revolution."[41]

Serving in Congress when Ellsworth did promised no mythic deliberations or historic resolutions. Although Congress no longer had to agree on matters as weighty as severing ties with the mother country, its members still had much—if not more—opportunity for disagreement and internal bickering. The exhilarating first steps of nationhood had given way to the long march of governance and the dizzying complexities of wartime administration. As the war continued, the sacrifices required of the individual states mounted. Yet the statesmen who shaped the early Congress had not been replaced by similar spokesmen for intercolonial union. "Very special gratitude and honor are due," Henry Cabot Lodge would explain in the tribute to Ellsworth that the Massachusetts senator delivered to the graduating students of the 1902 class of Yale Law School,

> to the few men of the first rank, like Ellsworth, who clung to [Congress] to the end, extorted from it the creation of certain rude executive departments, and forced it to the point of not alto-

gether abandoning Washington and the army. It was hard and thankless work not shining brilliantly before the eyes of men, but all the more to be honored because done in obscurity, in the midst of distrust and contempt, and without hope either of present applause or of future reward.[42]

The resulting discord that beset the wartime Congress convinced Ellsworth that patriots were needed now more than ever. The cause of independence was threatened with internal dissension as well as external attack. "It would be both more pleasing and more profitable to me to return home to my own family and business than to remain here any longer at this time," Ellsworth wrote his brother from Philadelphia in March 1780. "But you know when a soldier gets forth in public service he must stay until he is discharged, and though the weather be stormy and his allowance small yet still he must stand to his post." One month later, Ellsworth wrote his wife, explaining in similar terms why he could not leave his seat in Congress any time soon: "The public calamity & distress is at present too great for anyone to think of retiring from it who can be the least serviceable." Finally, in another letter to Abigail, written near the war's end, he explained once again the underlying purpose of his service to Congress. "Until the Storm was over," he wrote, "I could not desert the Ship or desert the post to which I was called for the public safety."[43]

Ellsworth was involved in two significant issues during his terms in Congress, which lasted until 1783. Both gave the young congressman a firsthand glimpse of the disharmony that had come to characterize relations between the several states. The political concerns Ellsworth addressed during these years—trivial and futile though they might have sometimes seemed—were the first steps in the project of founding a national government powerful enough to quell the discord between the states and bring instead a state of harmony between the separate parts of the American republic.

First Federal Courts

Beginning in 1778, Ellsworth served as a member of the Committee of Appeals, a five-member tribunal located in Congress and responsible for reviewing cases on appeal from state admiralty courts. As the first court established by America's national government with the authority to review cases that had been tried in state courts, the Committee of Appeals was a precursor to the United States Supreme Court. Present at the creation of the federal judiciary, Ellsworth was also there to witness its first misadventures.

A letter by General Washington led to the establishment of the Committee of Appeals. In the fall of 1775, a "Gale of Wind" sent a British ship carrying "120 Pipes of Wine" into an American port. Advised of the shipwreck, Washington wrote Congress to request that the delegates create a judicial system to determine what to do with the future booty that would fall into American hands. "These Accidents and Captures point out the necessity," wrote Washington, "of establishing proper Courts without loss of time for the decision of Property and the legality of Seizures." "Otherwise," warned Washington, "I may be Involved in inextricable difficulties."[44]

Soon after receiving Washington's letter, Congress agreed to a plan. Like the commander in chief, the delegates wanted to keep the conduct of Americans in wartime aboveboard. There would be no plundering. To this end, Congress took two steps: it encouraged the separate states to establish prize courts—the traditional venue for determining whether a captured vessel, cargo included, was lawfully taken—and it provided for an appeal to Congress in the event that a party disagreed with a state prize court. But Congress stopped short of creating a single prize court under the control of the federal government to try maritime suits.

Within a year, Congress received its first maritime suit on appeal. Shortly thereafter, Congress decided to create the standing Committee of Appeals, which was formally assigned the responsibility of reviewing state admiralty cases. In October 1778, when Ellsworth was selected to serve as one of the federal commissioners, the committee had decided thirty-eight cases on appeal.[45]

Within two months of Ellsworth's appointment, the question of the power of the state governments to restrict the committee's review authority came to a head. The particular dispute that triggered the controversy concerned a British sloop that sailed under the name *Active*. Gideon Olmstead and three other citizens of Connecticut had been captured by the British and impressed into service aboard the *Active*. Olmstead and his compatriots managed, however, to overthrow their captors. Upon taking command of the ship, the freed patriots made way for New York, where they hoped to dock the vessel. Before they safely arrived, the *Active* and its Connecticut crew were again captured, this time by Thomas Houston, who was the captain of a Pennsylvania brig. Captain Houston then took the British vessel into Philadelphia as the rightful prize of his ship and crew. A privateer cruising alongside Houston also claimed a share of the prize. Olmstead, meanwhile, claimed that the entire ship, which he had captured first, belonged to him.

The competing claims of the ship's various purported captors were all heard by the Pennsylvania Court of Admiralty, which the Pennsylvania General Assembly had recently established. The statute establishing this court provided that the Pennsylvania admiralty court was to consist of a civilian jury and a presiding judge. The civilian jury, moreover, was granted the authority to determine the facts of the case. Appeals were permitted from the admiralty courts only in cases where a party could show that the judge made a legal error during the trial. Under the Pennsylvania law creating the admiralty courts, factual errors by the jury could not be revisited.

At trial, the Pennsylvania jury awarded one-fourth of the prize to Olmstead, dividing the rest between Houston, the privateer, and the state of Pennsylvania. On appeal by Olmstead, the Committee of Appeals, which now included Ellsworth, overruled the decision by the Pennsylvania jury, determining instead that Olmstead was entitled to the entire prize. Following the appellate decision, however, George Ross, the Pennsylvania judge who had presided over the original trial, refused to enforce the committee's decree that the prize be sold and the proceeds directed to Olmstead. Judge Ross conceded that the Committee of Appeals had the power to set aside a legal ruling made by a state admiralty judge, but he deferred to the Pennsylvania law, which protected jury verdicts from further examination.

Ross, a signer of the Declaration of Independence, former member of the Continental Congress, and colonel in the Continental Army, died shortly after taking his stand against the Committee of Appeals. It would take nearly three decades for the Olmstead case to reach the U.S. Supreme Court. In 1809, Chief Justice John Marshall, also a veteran of Congress and the Continental Army, upheld the Committee of Appeals decision and delivered a stinging rebuke to the position held by Judge Ross. "If the legislatures of the several States may, at will, annul the judgments of the courts of the United States, and destroy the rights acquired under those judgments," opined Marshall, "the Constitution itself becomes a solemn mockery."[46]

In the immediate aftermath of Judge Ross's refusal to enforce the federal decree, Ellsworth joined three of his fellow commissioners in delivering to Congress a report containing the relevant proceedings in the *Active* case. Congress promptly created a committee to examine the federal government's jurisdiction in admiralty cases. Two months later, in March 1779, the committee returned with its recommendations. Its members agreed that "no finding of a jury in any court of admiralty . . . can or ought to destroy the right of appeal and the re-examination of the facts reserved to Congress." While Congress adopted the resolution, the delegates remained averse to establishing federal courts to hear admiralty suits. In August of the same year, however, Congress created another committee, charging this one "to report a plan for establishing one or more supreme courts of appeal in all maritime causes within these United States."[47]

The committee soon returned to Congress with a bold plan to create two courts of appeal with congressionally appointed judges, who would hear appeals without a jury and "according to the Civil Law, the law of nations and the usage and practice of the Courts of Admiralty in Europe," rather than the law of the state where the suit was first tried.[48] In January 1780, the delegates voted on a version of the committee's original recommendation that reduced the number of appellate courts to one but otherwise kept much of the proposal in place. The measure failed to gain a majority, but, in another effort toward a compromise, a new committee was created, which again included Ellsworth. Unlike its predecessor, the new committee succeeded in crafting a compromise that passed

Congress. The resolution created a three-judge panel authorized to hear cases in the federal capital of Philadelphia, as well as anywhere west of Hartford and north of Williamsburg. Litigants from outside this area would have to travel farther to have their day in the new appellate courts. In approving this resolution, Congress had instituted the first federal appellate courts, nearly a full decade before the ratification of the Constitution.[49]

As a member of the committee responsible for creating the early appellate courts for maritime suits, Oliver Ellsworth attempted to prevent these federal courts from undermining the sovereignty of local juries. The committee's recommendation, written in Ellsworth's hand, included a provision whereby delegates in the federal Congress officially advised their states to adopt a juryless practice for determining admiralty cases. This measure, clearly crafted to avoid future discord between local juries and the federal judges who ultimately heard admiralty cases on appeal, was ultimately adopted as part of the final resolution.[50]

At least two states, Pennsylvania and South Carolina, took Ellsworth's advice and barred juries from admiralty courts. Whether the committee's recommendation caused these states to change their practice is uncertain. Nevertheless, the strategy behind Ellsworth's recommendation was clear. Congress was in a difficult position, because when it began to exercise federal authority over admiralty cases in 1775, it had a carved a space for local jurors. (When it first asked the states to establish prize courts, Congress did not instruct them to make such courts juryless). As much as Congress expanded the federal government's power over admiralty decisions, the state juries stood in the way. As drafted by Ellsworth, the committee's approach was to expand the power of the central government, but only after gaining the approval of the states by asking them to remove citizen juries from admiralty courtrooms.[51]

Establishing federal courts to try admiralty cases—and simultaneously removing jurisdiction over the same suits from the states—was a more obvious way to grant the general government exclusive authority over such matters. Yet it is highly unlikely such a move would have then succeeded. The Articles of Confederation authorized Congress only to establish appellate courts to review admiralty disputes. The federal government was already struggling to raise sufficient funds to pay the Continental troops, straining relations between it and the states. Creating new courts would have been seen as an objectionable act of aggrandizement by the federal government.

When Ellsworth returned to Congress in 1789, the new Constitution had removed the earlier restriction that had permitted the Confederation Congress to establish only appellate review of admiralty courts. Article III of the Constitution, which set the limits of the federal government's judicial powers, allowed Congress to institute inferior courts over a range of cases, including admiralty disputes. Thus empowered, Ellsworth would complete the project of establishing a more perfect system of federal justice.

CURRENCY CRISIS

The struggle to maintain a valuable currency—the other political concern that captured Ellsworth's attention during his wartime service in Congress—further shaped Ellsworth's perspectives about the defects of the fledgling national government's structure. For Ellsworth and other early American political leaders, money was the sinew of war and constitutional change.

Throughout the eighteenth century, the colonies met their frequent military expenses through a system of currency finance. The system was designed to defray the costs of war while disrupting the local economy as little as possible. To avoid levying taxes, the colonies printed paper money, which was then distributed to soldiers and military suppliers. Because the currency was legal tender, it could be used for ordinary purchases and, as a result, circulated throughout the economy. Once the fighting ceased and the wartime expenses fell, the colony would retire the paper money by imposing taxes payable in the issued currency.

With the outbreak of the Revolutionary War, the colonists took the traditional funding path. In the three months following Lexington and Concord, Congress printed $2 million worth of paper money. By the end of 1775, the total reached $6 million. As military expenses increased, the wartime money machine continued to churn. By 1776, Congress had emitted $25 million in paper bills.

Ellsworth arrived in Philadelphia at a crucial moment in the Revolutionary experience with currency finance. After printing $13 million in 1777, Congress would circulate an additional $200 million over the next two years. As the supply grew, the value of the paper money plummeted. According to the records of one Philadelphia merchant, one dollar and twenty-five cents of the paper money could be exchanged for a dollar's worth of hard specie in January 1777. One year later, it took four paper dollars to acquire the same amount of specie. By October 1780, the exchange rate was thirty to one, and by January 1781, the rate had zoomed to one hundred to one.[52]

The critical financial issue that confronted Congress during Ellsworth's tenure was how the federal government would retire the large money debt. Prior to the Revolutionary War, the individual colonies had retired their own money debts through taxation. The Revolutionary debt was different because much of it had been issued by Congress. As had occurred with the paper money issued by individual colonies in the past, Congress provided for the acceptance of its "continentals" as legal tender, allowing holders to circulate the money freely throughout the states. But unlike the colonies that had issued paper money earlier, Congress had no legal power to tax individual citizens in order to retire the circulating debt. Under the Articles of Confederation, it had to rely upon the states to collect federal revenue. Herein lay the paper-money problem that confronted Ellsworth and his wartime colleagues in Congress. The federal government lacked the hard currency necessary to cover its expenses. Meanwhile, the paper money that it continued to print was becoming worthless. Without a reliable revenue stream, wartime superintendent of finance Robert Morris wryly concluded, the federal government would have to operate upon means "known only to Him who knoweth all things."[53]

Upon taking his seat in Congress, Ellsworth focused immediately on the falling value of the continentals. A month after arriving in Philadelphia, he sought to increase the national government's fiscal demands on the states. In January 1779, he introduced a resolution requesting that the states contribute a total of $15 million in the coming year, followed by an additional $6 million annually through 1795.[54] Acting on the idea, Congress adopted a nearly identical proposal. But the requisition failed to curb the currency's slide. In 1779, the states delivered less than $13 million in heavily depreciated dollars to the national treasury. During the same year, Congress printed more than $124 million in continentals, inundating the economy with increasingly worthless currency.[55]

Ellsworth was not finished with the currency puzzle. In March 1780, he offered another solution, which passed Congress by a single vote. Under this resolution, the states were asked to retire the entire supply of continentals. The novelty of the plan was that, unlike the requisitions that had been tried and failed, it offered the states an incentive to cooperate. Congress pledged to supply two dollars of a new currency to the states for every forty dollars of old continentals that they returned to the central government.

In a joint letter to governor of Connecticut Jonathan Trumbull, written on the day Congress adopted the measure, Ellsworth and his Connecticut colleague Roger Sherman explained the rationale behind the new currency plan. In place of the existing continentals, wrote the Connecticut delegates, the plan created new paper bills that would be more valuable because of "the smallness of the quantity to be in circulation." The measure also shortened the terms of the new bills, provided funds for their redemption, and promised annual interest payments to their holders—all tools designed to create further support for the replacement currency.[56]

The intention of the new plan was to entice the states to retire the existing currency. Since the new issue was expected to be more valuable than the circulating continentals, the states were encouraged to retire as many of the old bills as possible so as to receive in return a larger supply of the new issue. "Hastily written as their letter doubtless was," one Ellsworth biographer concluded of the Ellsworth-Sherman report, "dry and matter-of-fact though it is, one might search long without finding another contemporary document, unless it should be some letter of Robert Morris himself, setting forth more correctly the state of the finances at this time and the actual working of that side of the new government."[57]

However deferential it was to the states, Ellsworth's plan did not reverse the depreciation of the Continental currency. By 1781, Congress had decided upon a bolder course of action, formally requesting that the states amend the Articles of Confederation to permit a 5 percent federal tax on imported goods. Still, Ellsworth's failed currency plan represents an important moment in his early political career because it demonstrates Ellsworth's willingness to change his views to align them with what he understood as God's overall plan—the Almighty's "grand and glorious scheme" of which his boyhood tutor Reverend Bellamy had so often preached. Prior to recommending his plan, Ellsworth had publicly decried the replacement of the circulating Continental currency at less than face value. On January 20, 1779, Ellsworth had published his "Thoughts on the Paper Currency" in a Hartford newspaper. Therein the young congressman warned that officially depreciating the nation's paper money "would be madness, atheism and suicide." A year later, Ellsworth adopted the very position that he had recently opposed. Ellsworth explained his reversal on the grounds that God's larger plan was for the American Revolution to succeed. If God's overall scheme was for an independent America, its leaders were justified—if not required—to adopt the necessary policies, even if it meant that the government had to renege on its full obligations to holders of Continental money. "The continental treasury is now empty," Ellsworth wrote to Connecticut's Governor Trumbull in March 1780.

> This has been nearly the case for some weeks. The consequence is that the continental agents have not only discontinued their purchases, but cannot move forward the little supplies they have on hand; and the army are [sic] again in want. Nor does it yet appear when either the army or Treasury will be supplied by the several States. Surely, Sir, they do not expect the war to be carried on without means, nor can they mean to let it drop here. Does it

not then behoove them to adopt effectual measures for drawing forth their resources, and that without a moment's delay? Can it, Sir, be the design of Heaven, that has roused us to exertions thus far, and armed mighty nations for our support and brought us within sight of the promised rest, to leave us after all to destruction, and to lament also the best blood of our land as spilt in vain? I trust not.[58]

PATH TO PHILADELPHIA

By the end of his tenure in the wartime Congress, Oliver Ellsworth had come to believe that individual states needed to cede some of their authority—in this case, over the federal government's ability to raise money—in order to provide for the "common defense" of all the states. Three years after his currency plan failed, Ellsworth voted in favor of a renewed effort to grant the federal government a revenue stream that did not have to pass through the state governments.[59] Following this vote, Ellsworth turned his attention to the next battle. Since the resolution required amending the Articles of Confederation, it needed to be approved by every state (as was the rule for modifying the Articles).

In a letter to Connecticut's governor, Ellsworth explained the reasons why this constitutional change was mandated. "There must, Sir," he wrote,

be a revenue somehow established that can be relied on & applied for national purposes as the exigencies arise, independent of the will or views of a single State, or it will be impossible to support national faith or national existence. The powers of Congress should be defined, but their means must be adequate to the purposes of their institutions. It is possible there may be abuses & misapplications—still it is better to hazard something than to hazard all.[60]

When Congress had previously passed resolutions to amend the Articles to permit federal taxation of individuals, Connecticut's generally pronationalist legislature had consented to the constitutional change.[61] But this time the political winds had shifted, handing Ellsworth a stinging setback. Returning to Connecticut's General Assembly, where he had a seat in the upper chamber, Ellsworth drafted the necessary legislation that would have given his state's assent to the congressional resolution. Connecticut's lower house voted down the measure.

Within months of Connecticut's negative vote, popular opposition to the taxing measure would subside. Meanwhile, Connecticut's legislature prohibited plural officeholding, prompting Ellsworth to retire from the upper chamber to fill the seat he had recently been appointed to on the state's Superior Court.[62]

Ellsworth left Congress in 1783. Two years later, he departed the Connecticut General Assembly. Yet his stature within Connecticut did not fade. In May 1787, Connecticut's General Assembly would select Ellsworth to represent the state at the Constitutional Convention.[63]

Although he had not been among the reformers who called for a Constitutional Convention to correct the defects of the Articles, Ellsworth was committed to a principle crucial to the Convention's ultimate success—namely, the conviction that a balance be struck between state and federal power, one that would maintain the principle of local rule while also creating a general government strong enough to preserve the harmony of the republic.

CHAPTER THREE

THE ELECTORAL FEDERALIST

Let not too much be attempted by which all may be lost.

—Oliver Ellsworth, June 29, 1787

"This Noble Attempt"

In May 1787, four years after leaving the Confederation Congress, Oliver Ellsworth returned to Philadelphia to attend the Constitutional Convention. The Convention marks an eventful, if stunningly brief, chapter in the life of Ellsworth. In a single summer, the forty-two-year-old, Windsor-born attorney and his colleagues drafted a new plan for the nation's government. Connecticut's Governor Samuel Huntington, with whom Ellsworth would argue the case for the Constitution before Connecticut's ratifying convention, summarized the achievement of the framers. "Never before," remarked Huntington, "did a people, in time of peace and tranquility, meet together by their representatives, and with calm deliberation frame for themselves a system of government. This noble attempt does honor to our country."[1]

Among the fifty-five luminaries who participated in the Convention, Ellsworth's fellow delegates James Madison and Alexander Hamilton are sometimes considered the "fathers of the Constitution," though it may be more accurate to say that Hamilton and Madison are the fathers of the Convention, not the Constitution itself. In September 1786, Hamilton and Madison gathered in Annapolis with delegates from five states. Most likely at Madison's bidding, the Virginia legislature had proposed the meeting for the purpose of adopting a uniform code of interstate commercial regulations. At Annapolis, Madison and Hamilton persuaded their colleagues to seek Congress's approval for another convention to meet in Philadelphia on the second Monday in May.[2] In February 1787, Congress authorized "a Convention of delegates . . . for the sole and express purpose of revising the Articles of Confederation."[3]

Although Madison and Hamilton were, in large part, responsible for the assemblage of the delegates, the Constitution that came from the Convention did not ultimately resemble the plans that Madison and Hamilton favored in Philadelphia. Madison lost forty of the seventy-one proposals that he either made or endorsed at the Convention.[4] Moreover, the manner in which the new government would have operated under Madison's plan differed in several critical ways from the framers' final plan. The Virginia delegate recommended that the House of Representatives elect the Senate (rejected for election by state legislatures); that the president be elected by Congress (rejected for election by the Electoral College); and that Congress be empowered to veto all state laws that were, in Congress's opinion, unconstitutional (rejected for the retroactive process of adjudication in the federal courts).[5]

When Hamilton, "hitherto silent," took the floor on June 18 to unveil over the course of a five- to six-hour-long speech his plan for a new American government, directed by a lifetime president and a legislature "with power to pass all laws whatsoever," the delegates ignored him.[6] Hamilton would depart the Convention on June 29. In his return address to the delegates on September 6 (apart from a brief stay in Philadelphia in August, the delegate had been home in New York since June), Hamilton wasted little time before registering his "dislike of the Scheme of Govt. in General." The waning days of the Convention did nothing to lift Hamilton's mood. Of the framers' finished product, the New Yorker vented that "no man's ideas were more remote from the plan than his."[7]

In actuality, the hard compromises that produced the Constitution were quite often the handiwork of lesser-known delegates, among them Oliver Ellsworth of Connecticut.

"Connecticut Held a Middle Rank"

Ellsworth's most important contribution to the Convention was the role that he played in achieving the "Connecticut Compromise," the agreement that continues to provide each state with the same number of seats in the Senate. For the first month of the Convention, debate over this question consumed more time than any other issue. The delegates assigned great significance to the proper formula for apportioning seats in the new Congress. The experience under the Articles of Confederation had made it clear to them that the federal government needed additional powers. But before the delegates could agree to provide it with the power to tax, spend, regulate commerce, and raise armies, they had to decide how the new federal government would be composed. For proponents of a stronger national government, such as Hamilton, Madison, and James Wilson of Pennsylvania, giving the states an equal voice in Congress threatened the enactment of genuinely national policies. For Ellsworth, the equal representation of the states at the national level was necessary to maintain national harmony.

It is true that on the question of whether to apportion senators by population or equally to each state regardless of its population, the delegates voted largely in blocs, according to the size of their home state's population. The large-state bloc was anchored by the delegates of the two most populous states—Virginia (747,000 inhabitants) and Pennsylvania (433,000)—while the small-state bloc included the smallest state, Delaware (60,000), and its neighbor New Jersey (154,000), both of whose delegations were outspoken that the equality of the states was essential to any new plan of government. But the delegates had other considerations, too. Though having only 82,000 inhabitants, Georgia voted initially with the large-state bloc, driven perhaps by the estimation that the state's population would increase sizably due to the continued importation of African slaves.[8]

Sectional suspicions—more than population size alone—may have also persuaded certain states to favor equal state apportionment. The concern that neighboring Virginia, allied perhaps with the slave-importing, and thus consistently growing, South Carolina, was poised to dominate the union under a plan of popular apportionment may have weighed on the minds of the Maryland delegates who voted for equal state apportionment despite representing a state with 319,000 inhabitants. Connecticut's 237,000 inhabitants placed Ellsworth's home state just behind South Carolina (249,000), one of the pillars of the large-state bloc. Yet Connecticut's delegates may have been worried specifically about its more populous neighbors New York (340,000 and rapidly increasing) and Massachusetts (378,000) combining their votes to control the nation's commercial policies at the expense of Connecticut, which, lacking a natural port, was forced to rely on Manhattan and Boston to sell its agricultural surplus and purchase imports.[9] The impost that the state of New York levied on the goods that arrived at its ports was a particular sore spot to residents of Connecticut prior to the enactment of the Constitution. In defending the framers' plan in the pages of the *Connecticut Courant*, Ellsworth made it a point to remind his state's readers of the harm that New York's self-interested public policies had been inflicting upon her sister states. "In New York the opposition is not to this constitution in particular, but to the federal impost, it is confined wholly to salary-men and their connections, men whose salary is paid by the state impost. This class of citizens," continued Ellsworth, "are endeavoring to convince the ignorant part of the community that an annual income of fifty thousand pounds, extorted from the citizens of Massachusetts, Connecticut and New Jersey, is a great blessing to the state of New York."[10] At the dawn of the Convention, there was little harmony between states.

Not least were the delegates motivated by their respective visions for the future republic. New York's Robert Yates and John Lansing, Maryland's Luther Martin, and Elbridge Gerry of Massachusetts opposed popular apportionment primarily because they did not want to alter, in any fundamental way, the confederation of states that was in place under the Articles of Confederation.[11] To a considerable extent, the debate over the apportionment of the Senate was over theoretical concerns, specifically, how to represent the American people. The arguments that Madison and James Wilson of Pennsylvania, in particular, staked in favor of popular apportionment were constructed with the view in mind that a national legislature needed to represent the people, and not their states. That Madison and Wilson returned so frequently to this theoretical view that governments gained legitimacy only through the popular apportionment of the public's representatives demonstrates that these leading spokesmen for popular apportionment were principally concerned with matters that transcended whether their home states would be victorious in certain early congressional votes. Similarly, Ellsworth, in his defense of representing the states equally in the Senate, looked beyond the immediate concerns of his home state, noting, in one floor speech, that his perspective on the matter was "not the result of partial or local views" since the "State he represented [Connecticut] held a middle rank."[12]

"I Never Saw Two Men More Alike"

The battle lines for the apportionment debate were drawn at the onset of the proceedings when, on May 29, Virginia delegate Edmund Randolph put forth the Virginia Plan. Although presented by Randolph for practical considerations—Randolph was then governor of the largest state in the Confederation, a forceful speaker, and nearly as tall as the Convention's most esteemed attendee, General Washington—the Virginia Plan had been drawn by James Madison.[13] It proposed to replace the existing constitution entirely. Under the Virginia Plan, Congress would be restructured into a bicameral chamber whose seats were apportioned according either to the amount that each state contributed to the treasury or the size of its population. Under the Articles, each state had possessed the same single vote on all matters that came before Congress. Two weeks into the Convention, on June 11, a majority of states approved a measure that provided for popular apportionment in the House. The vote was seven to three, with Maryland's delegates divided.[14] (At the Convention, each state cast a single vote on all proposals. A total of eleven states were present for the votes on apportionment due to Rhode Island's boycott of the Convention and the midsummer arrival of New Hampshire's delegates, John Langdon and Nicholas Gilman, who had waited months for their home state to finance their mission to Philadelphia before Langdon reached into his own coffers to defray the delegation's expenses. Ours was once a start-up republic.)[15]

Ellsworth joined his fellow Connecticut delegates Roger Sherman and William Samuel Johnson to side with the majority of states in favor of popular apportionment, but when Sherman used the passage of this measure to move that each state be allocated the same one vote "in the second branch of the National Legislature," Ellsworth seconded the Sherman proposal for an equal state vote in the Senate.[16]

The Connecticut Compromise was most likely Roger Sherman's idea. It was Sherman who, on June 11, offered the first floor speech at the Convention in favor of the proposition that a middle ground could be found if seats in the House were apportioned according to the formula favored by large states, while seats in the Senate were apportioned according to the formula favored by small states.[17] But from the moment that Sherman proposed the Connecticut Compromise, Ellsworth signaled his support. On June 11, Ellsworth voted—along with Sherman—both in favor of popular apportionment in the House and in favor of equal state apportionment in the Senate.

While it was Sherman who initiated the Connecticut Compromise, Ellsworth emerged as the proposal's principal spokesman. In this way, Sherman and Ellsworth operated like a team—with Sherman planting the seeds of a possible middle way and Ellsworth, the seasoned litigator, taking on the role of persuader in chief. This is probably no accident.

The Massachusetts-born son of a shoemaker, Sherman was, at age sixty-six, the second-oldest delegate, behind Benjamin Franklin. Although a lawyer and almanac publisher, Sherman, to a greater extent than perhaps any delegate, was known professionally for the public offices that he had held throughout his adult life. Within Connecticut, he had been a member of both houses of Connecticut's Assembly, a justice of the peace, a justice of the county court, and a judge of the state Superior Court, as well as a tax collector, town clerk, and Congregationalist deacon. He was also a regular delegate to Congress, who, in the course of his federal service, had put his signature to the Articles of Association (the document of the 1774 Continental Congress protesting Great Britain's tightening of colonial administration), the Declaration of Independence, the Articles of Confederation, and the 1783 peace treaty with Great Britain. Arguably no delegate had the same depth of experience in the art of early American politics as Roger Sherman.[18]

Sherman and Ellsworth voted together 80 percent of the time at the Convention.[19] Religiously, both were New Light Calvinists. Politically, both were Federalists, who favored a stronger general government. In his almanac from 1753, Sherman offered his readers a slogan that previewed the future officeholder's ideological leanings: "Liberty & Property are Dear to Englishmen."[20] Up through the Convention, Sherman worked diligently to secure the claims that Connecticut's residents had made upon a swath of land west of Pennsylvania.[21] As a good Whig of eighteenth-century Lockean proclivities, Sherman maintained that legislatures were designed to protect the rights of property holders and thus ought to be the most powerful branch of any government. But Sherman was more a conciliator than an ideologue. He had a sense of the politician as needing to create a consensus that reflected the greatest good that was possible, even if it conflicted with some of what his constituents desired. After Sherman's death, Yale president Timothy Dwight commented that the Connecticut politician "had no fashionable opinions, and could never be persuaded to swim with the tide. Independent of everything but argument, he judged for himself; and rarely failed to convince others that he judged right."[22]

Raised in the same political soil, Sherman and Ellsworth shared an instinct for compromise, though years of formal study under New Light theologians had given Ellsworth additionally a deep-seated theological motivation for seeking national harmony. Observers noticed that the two Connecticut delegates had much in common. After describing "Monsieur Ellsworth" as "a man simple in his manners, but wise and infinitely reasonable," G. W. Otto, the French chargé d'affaires who sent several astute dispatches of the Convention to his home government, commented that the same could be said of Sherman. "The people of that state have in general," concluded Otto, "a national character that is seldom found in other parts of the continent. They clothe themselves with the greatest republican simplicity; they are all comfortable without knowing opulence."[23]

Their critical differences were in age and appearance. Ellsworth viewed Sherman, twenty-four years his senior, as his political mentor. To John Adams, Ellsworth would later remark that "he had made Mr. Sherman his model in his youth."[24] But Sherman's understudy possessed certain gifts that the elder politician lacked. Unlike Ellsworth, who had attended Yale and Princeton, Sherman was largely self-taught. As Adams would write of the Connecticut duo, "I never saw two men more alike except that [Ellsworth] had the advantage of liberal education, and somewhat more extensive reading."[25] And unlike the tall and robust Ellsworth, who stood confidently on his feet and readily commanded the attention of juries and assemblies alike, Sherman was physically unimpressive. By Dwight's account, Ellsworth was "formed to be a great man."[26] "The reverse of grace" was how Adams described Sherman, despite admiring him. Delegate William Pierce of Georgia, who included vignettes of each of the delegates in his journal, depicted Sherman as "the oddest shaped character I ever remember," "awkward," and "unaccountably strange in his manner." Sherman also spoke with what Pierce called "a New England cant" that made "everything that is connected with him grotesque and laughable." Ellsworth, on the other hand, was capable of "floods of eloquence which were irresistible and overwhelming," according to Yale president Dwight. "When Ellsworth rose," concurred John Trumbull, "the jury soon began to drop their heads, and, winking, looked up through their eyebrows, while his eloquence seemed to drive every idea into their very skulls in spite of them."[27] With Sherman possessing experience and Ellsworth a commanding presence, the two Connecticut delegates neatly complemented each other. (The state's third delegate, William Samuel Johnson, a Federalist lawyer widely regarded for his erudition, fit in well with the delegation).

Ellsworth would eclipse Sherman in influence. Following the Constitutional Convention, Ellsworth, not Sherman, served as the principal spokesman in support of the Constitution at Connecticut's ratification convention. Connecticut's legislature chose Ellsworth to represent the state in the First Senate. Sherman would take a seat in Congress. But never was there a hint of envy between them. Sherman and Ellsworth maintained instead a close friendship throughout their careers. Prior to the Convention, they had served together as judges on Connecticut's Superior Court. During the Convention, they both lodged at Mrs. Marshall's boarding house on Second Street. Whenever in New Haven, Ellsworth routinely paid his respects at Sherman's grave after the Connecticut statesman's death in 1793.[28]

"Partly National, Partly Federal"

Whether or not Sherman and Ellsworth coordinated their efforts, it is clear from the records of the Convention that after Sherman proposed the idea, Ellsworth would be largely responsible for articulating the rationale for the Connecticut Compromise. On June 11, when Sherman and Ellsworth voted in favor of popular apportionment in the House of Representatives and, in a separate vote pursuant to Sherman's motion, for state-based apportionment in the Senate, the Connecticut delegates signaled that they favored moderate change and the protection of small-state interests. At this stage in the Convention, however, Sherman was not able to convince a majority of delegates to support the compromise that he had now proposed. It would take several weeks for the Connecticut delegates to build a majority for their compromise plan.

The immediate reaction to the Sherman-Ellsworth motion for equal apportionment in the Senate was a counterproposal from James Wilson and Hamilton calling for popular apportionment in this chamber. Six states against five rejected the Sherman measure, opting for the Wilson-Hamilton alternative. (At this point in the Convention, the delegates convened as a Committee of the Whole, a parliamentary device that allowed them to debate and vote on the various measures without the final vote at the committee counting as the Convention's ultimate word on the measure.) Despite the early defeat of Sherman's motion, the issue remained alive due to the fervor among advocates of the equal state vote. Once again, it was Sherman who took the early lead in advancing the Connecticut Compromise. Raising his motion, the veteran Connecticut politician insisted that "everything depended" on the equality of suffrage in the Senate. "The smaller States," warned Sherman, "would never agree to the plan on any other principle."[29]

The question of Senate apportionment was further delayed when William Paterson of New Jersey introduced a new draft constitution on June 15. Paterson's proposal (dubbed the New Jersey Plan) increased the power of Congress by authorizing it to raise revenue through a tariff on imports and to regulate foreign commerce. But Paterson proposed to maintain basic elements of the existing Confederation. Under the New Jersey Plan, each state would have one vote in Congress, just as under the Articles.[30] During the consideration of the New Jersey Plan, the Connecticut delegates again indicated through their vote that they wanted to modify the existing system. On June 19, Connecticut joined a majority of states (the final tally was seven to three, with Maryland's delegates divided) in dismissing the New Jersey Plan and voting to "re-report" the Virginia Plan.[31]

When the Virginia Plan had last been discussed, prior to the debate over the New Jersey Plan, the delegates had yet to resolve the question of apportioning seats in the second house of the proposed Congress. In the final week of June, debate over Senate apportionment resumed, with Ellsworth now taking the floor as a strong proponent of the equal state vote.

Ellsworth's opening volley in the Senate apportionment debate came on June 25, when he rose to respond to James Wilson's exhortation against giving the state governments any role in the election of congressmen on the grounds that the central government "is not an assemblage of states, but of individuals for certain political purposes," and therefore "the individuals . . . not the States, ought to be represented in it."[32] Relying upon the political tenet, articulated by the eighteenth-century French aristocrat Montesquieu and widely held among the delegates, that large republics were ungovernable, Ellsworth argued that the vast size of the American republic made "co-operation" between the state and general government essential. According to Ellsworth, the recent political turmoil in Massachusetts, where rebels, whose ranks included a large number of former Continental Army officers, succeeded in shutting down five state courts, illustrated that the mere presence of a central government would not be sufficient to provide for the safety of the nation's population, already dispersed over thirteen states and expected to spread farther west. "The largest states are the Worst Governed," Ellsworth told the delegates. "Massachusetts could not keep the peace one hundred miles from her capitol," he said, referring to the state's uprising, since memorialized as Shays's Rebellion after the former army captain Daniel Shays, who commanded the largest regiment of Massachusetts insurgents.[33] However perfectly they organized the federal government on paper, Ellsworth was reminding the delegates, the plan would still have to work in practice. Governments rarely work according to mechanistic principles. Plans for human institutions, as governments always are, must factor in ambition and self-interest. Without the state governments, Ellsworth further advised, the general government would have to wield excessive power if it wanted to control an area as large as the United States. Ellsworth agreed with nationalist-minded reformers that a stronger federal government was necessary. But to assist the federal government, he looked to the state governments, authorities that were already familiar to the American people. "The only chance of supporting a General Government," he asserted, "lies in engrafting it on that of the individual States."[34]

Four days later, Ellsworth used the passage of another resolution guaranteeing population-based suffrage in the House to redouble his effort. With popular sovereignty secure in one chamber, the next step was to protect state sovereignty in the other. The time was ripe for a compromise. Taking the floor, Ellsworth asserted one of the Convention's most memorable lines. Its clarity prodded the delegates to accept the prudent settlement before them. Referring to the nation, Ellsworth intoned, "We were partly national, partly federal." The dual citizenship of the American people harmonized with the dual system of apportionment that Ellsworth favored. Proportional representation in the House was "comfortable to the national principle," he explained, while "an equality of voices" in the Senate "was comfortable to the federal principle."[35] Ellsworth was not content to rest upon this neat symmetry. "If no compromise should take place," he added, "our meeting would not only be in vain but worse than vain."[36] Deprived of equal representation, many states would leave the union. The incorporation of the states into the federal government—and not their wholesale subjugation to such a government—was needed to achieve the central mission of the Convention: a more powerful union. "Let a strong Executive, a Judiciary and Legislative power be created," Ellsworth concluded, "but let not too much be attempted by which all may be lost."[37]

Ellsworth displayed his rhetorical skill by fashioning a straightforward message: accept the equal state vote in the Senate or risk the disintegration of the nation; in other words, union or no union, national harmony or quite possibly confederate sectionalism. Courtroom experience had taught the attorney-delegate to condense a complex debate into a single question and then to repeat the obvious answer to his audience. James Madison, whom Ellsworth ultimately bettered in the apportionment debate, later praised the directness with which his erstwhile colleague presented his views. "As a speaker," recalled Madison, "his reasoning was clear and close and delivered in a style and tone which rendered it emphatic and impressive."[38] Georgia delegate William Pierce, who frequently aired his critiques of his fellow delegates in the pages of his journal, was similarly impressed. "Mr. Ellsworth is a . . . Gentlemen of clear, deep, and copious understanding," wrote Pierce, adding that Ellsworth was "eloquent, and connected in public debate."[39]

Another factor behind the success of Ellsworth's case for the equal state vote in the Senate was that, notwithstanding the common misperception, it had little to do with states' rights. Early in the Convention, Ellsworth split with Sherman on the question of whether Congress should be permitted to exercise lawmaking authority over "all cases to which the State Legislatures were individually incompetent." Sherman voted no, while Ellsworth registered his support of the proposal, which would have stopped short of specifying—and thereby further limiting—Congress's powers. Unlike Sherman, Ellsworth was from the younger generation of American leaders, whose formative political experiences (the War for Independence followed by the crisis of the Articles of Confederation) had led them to favor a greater degree of centralization. By contrast, older political hands such as Sherman had loyalties to their states that predated, by several decades in Sherman's case, the era in which gatherings among the various leaders of the states became regular.[40]

But Ellsworth, unlike Madison, Hamilton, and other pro-nationalist delegates who came of political age during the Revolution, also believed that it was possible to have a powerful federal government that represented the states equally. On at least one point, Ellsworth was correct. The allocation of seats in the federal Senate said nothing of the powers that the federal government could exercise or the extent to which the states might govern themselves free from federal supervision. On the contrary, the equal state vote in the Senate was then—and remains today—more precisely a question of states' representation than states' rights.

Ellsworth was not the only delegate who saw that it was possible to strengthen the general government while also protecting the equal state vote. Charles Cotesworth Pinckney of South Carolina predicted that New Jersey would "concur in the National system" provided that it had an "equal vote."[41] After the defeat of the New Jersey Plan, Ellsworth emerged as the leading spokesman for the compromise. Nationalists would gain a stronger federal government in return for the equal state vote in the Senate. Since Ellsworth favored both, the bargain suited him well. "So I received it from the lips of Madison," commented the nineteenth-century historian George Bancroft, the smaller states "exceeded all others in zeal for granting powers to the general government" once the equal state vote was secure. "Ellsworth," Bancroft continued, "became one of [the general government's] strongest pillars."[42]

On the final day of June, Ellsworth and James Wilson locked horns for one last bout over equal apportionment. Speaking first, the Scottish-born Wilson returned to his core claim. State-based suffrage was antidemocratic. "Can we forget for whom we are forming a government," queried the Pennsylvania delegate. "Is it for men, or for imaginary beings called States?"[43] Ellsworth began his last rebuttal by objecting to Wilson's claim that the equal state vote in the Senate amounted to minority rule. The states would have equal representation only in the Senate, not the entire Congress. Turning the fear that states would collude back at proponents of full popular apportionment, Ellsworth argued that the equal state vote in the Senate ensured that the larger states would not combine their votes in the popularly based House to protect their own interests. "Suppose that in pursuance of some commercial treaty or arrangement three or four free ports & no more were to be established," said Ellsworth. "Would not combinations be formed in favor of Boston, Philadelphia, and some port in [the] Chesapeake?"[44]

For the Connecticut delegate, the effect of the equal Senate vote was a harmonious constitution, not minority rule. He compared this arrangement with the British system, where the aristocratic House of Lords could veto the perceived excesses of the popularly based House of Commons. The lords "cannot give away the property of the community," noted Ellsworth, "but they can prevent the commons from being too lavish in their gifts." That "so many gentlemen have united in applauding" Britain's balanced constitution proved Ellsworth's point.[45] A purely popular government amounted to a dangerous leap of faith. "Mankind is apt to go from one extreme to another," he warned his colleagues. "We are raising the foundations of the building when we need only to repair the roof."[46]

Ellsworth maintained that the arrangement also provided the best answer to another critical question. Throughout the Revolution, the delegates and their countrymen had criticized Britain's Parliament in part because it did not formally represent the American people. Among Americans, the protest elevated the principle that all laws required the consent of the people. The quest for a new constitution forced the delegates to decide how to guarantee representation of the American people at the national level.

From Ellsworth's perspective, to achieve national harmony the framers needed to recognize that the unity of the American people existed on two levels: among the people as Americans and among their separate states. As he had succinctly remarked, the American people were "partly national" and "partly federal." Both identities deserved representation. Notably, one of Ellsworth's chief adversaries on apportionment publicly adopted his approach in the aftermath of the Constitutional Convention. Using Ellsworth's exact words, James Madison concluded one of his best-known *Federalist* essays by noting that the sources of the new government's powers were "partly federal and partly national."[47]

After establishing himself as an advocate for equal apportionment, Ellsworth's next move involved the use of the parliamentary skills that he had honed on the floors of the Connecticut legislature and in the halls of the Revolutionary Congress. On the morning of July 2, he seized the opportunity to call another vote on apportioning seats in the Senate. It is likely that Ellsworth timed the motion to bolster its chances of passing. When the vote was taken, Maryland delegate Daniel of St. Thomas Jenifer was absent. Jenifer, who was late in arriving at the convention hall that day, had supported popular apportionment. With his absence, and with Maryland's remaining delegate, Luther Martin, supporting the equal state apportionment in the Senate, another state would vote "aye."[48] While Ellsworth correctly predicted Maryland's vote, his motion still fell short. The final tally was five against five, with one state, Georgia, registering a mixed vote. The nation's delegates were divided down the middle. "We are now at a full stop," commented Sherman, who promptly moved for a committee of eleven delegates—one from each state represented—to settle the matter.[49]

The compilation of the committee demonstrated that the proponents of the equal state vote had prevailed at last. Of the eleven committeemen chosen, vocal supporters of equal state suffrage noticeably outnumbered committed proponents of popular apportionment. Anti-Federalists Elbridge Gerry of Massachusetts, Luther Martin of Maryland, George Mason of Virginia, and Robert Yates of New York were chosen to represent their respective states.[50] Although initially nominated to represent Connecticut, Ellsworth was "kept away by indisposition," in Madison's words, allowing Sherman to take his place on the committee.[51]

The morning after Independence Day, the committee returned, having agreed on the details of what would become known as the Connecticut Compromise. Proponents of state-based suffrage received equal representation in the Senate, while the popularly based House gained the power to initiate all tax and spending legislation. Two weeks later, the arrangement became official when North Carolina's delegation cast its support for the plan, breaking the deadlock that had previously prevented a resolution.[52] The long debate had ended. The new Congress would be "partly national" and "partly federal." Ellsworth must have been pleased with the prospects for future harmony. His determination throughout the rest of the Convention to preserve the agreed-to framework for the new government makes this clear.

Old Wine, New Skins

Following the apportionment debate, the delegates nominated Ellsworth to serve on the five-member Committee of Detail. The committee's mission was to construct a single, coherent plan from the many constitutional provisions and resolutions that had been drafted. In late July, the Convention took leave for ten days as the committee gathered. When delegates reassembled on August 6, they were each given a copy of the drafting committee's final product. At seven pages in length, and divided into twenty-three articles, the document described the particular powers that would be given to the three distinct branches of the federal government. The committeemen had delivered the first draft of the Constitution.

Shortly after the release of the draft constitution, the delegates considered several provisions that concerned the qualifications necessary for congressional candidates and voters. Like the apportionment question, debates over congressional membership and voter eligibility had the potential to affect all areas of national policy. The requirements for holding congressional office determined who would have the authority to legislate in all areas within Congress's powers. It was often the case at the Convention that the most heated debates were over the process by which the American political system would operate. The delegates largely agreed that the federal government needed the power to raise armies, tax, regulate interstate commerce, and conduct foreign policy—all of which were written into the Constitution.[53] They also understood that the procedures they set for the new government would affect the outcomes of virtually all future debates. For instance, constitutionally barring debtors from holding federal office would predictably shape the nation's bankruptcy laws. Likewise, limiting the franchise in federal elections to large property owners might make future Congresses less willing to sympathize with the desire of the middling classes to facilitate the settlement of western lands. Then as now, personnel was policy.

With respect to the provisions that would dictate how the new federal offices would be filled, Ellsworth advanced a view that might be called electoral federalism. While other framers favored setting strict national standards for matters such as the eligibility for voting in congressional elections, Ellsworth supported giving local constituents wide discretion over the rules that would determine who would participate in the nation's political life. In the face of pressure by nationalist delegates for the creation of a centrally regulated political marketplace, Ellsworth advanced a locally regulated one.

Ellsworth's electoral federalism once again illustrates the type of harmony that he wished to see the young nation achieve. The federal government needed to be powerful enough to bring a wayward state—or minority of states—into line. At the same time, true to his Connecticut Congregationalist roots, Ellsworth maintained that national government needed to represent smaller communities, which, like the towns and church congregations of Connecticut, deserved wide latitude in the selection of the leaders they chose to represent them.

Not all the delegates shared either Ellsworth's New Light–influenced politics or his resulting electoral federalism. The disputes over congressional officeholding and voting requirements pitted Ellsworth against the same delegates who had opposed the equal state vote in the Senate, including James Wilson and James Madison, further clarifying what was truly at stake in the apportionment question. These additional debates reveal Ellsworth's vision of a harmonious national government whose officers remained close to local constituencies. They also show the alternate—and ultimately unsuccessful—vision of a government that would have greatly distanced itself from the American people in order to govern them effectively.

The discussion of eligibility rules for voting in congressional elections provided the first opportunity for Ellsworth to explain his broader view of the national legislature's proper composition. On the day after the delegates reconvened to consider the Committee of Detail's draft constitution, Ellsworth was compelled to defend the committee's method for determining the eligibility of voters in congressional elections against objections that the committee's provision was too permissive. The drafting committee had proposed that anyone eligible to vote in elections for state lawmakers be eligible to vote in congressional elections. State lawmakers would determine who among their state's citizens could vote in federal elections. This promoted broad voter participation. The only way to restrict voter eligibility in congressional races was to restrict the ability of voters to participate in elections for their own state's legislature. As it would be unpopular for any state legislature to enact overly restrictive requirements for choosing local representatives, the draft provision had the effect of encouraging—without mandating—a large electorate in congressional contests.[54]

Pennsylvania delegate Gouverneur Morris immediately objected to what he considered overly lenient suffrage requirements. He moved to make what he called "the main object of society"— property—a requisite for congressional voting. Morris offered a provision that "would restrain the right of suffrage to freeholders." The proposal produced a practical objection from James Wilson, who had served with Ellsworth on the drafting committee. Wilson pointed out that voters who did not own freehold estates would likely be upset if, on Election Day, they were allowed to choose their state representatives but not their federal ones. Undeterred, Morris retorted that "such a hardship would neither be great nor novel." State voters were already accustomed to being eligible to choose certain state officers but not others.[55]

Morris's response may have answered Wilson's objection, but it failed to satisfy Ellsworth. "The people," said Ellsworth, "will not readily subscribe to the National Constitution if it should subject them to be disfranchised." The ringing reply again illustrated Ellsworth's ability to leave his audience with a memorable summary of his perspective. The experienced litigator's point was simple: the delegates had to remember their goal. Their work would have to be adopted by the American people.[56]

The prospect of ratification was not all that was on Ellsworth's mind. Otherwise he might have given further consideration to Morris's claim that limiting suffrage to freeholders was politically feasible when "9/10 of the Inhabitants are Freeholders." The Connecticut delegate had another reason for favoring the draft constitution's provision, one which was related more closely to the electoral federalism that he favored. After all, what the delegates were debating was not simply whether property ownership should be required for congressional voting but, more fundamentally, who was in the best position to decide what qualified an individual to choose federal officers. Delegates such as Morris believed that the framers themselves ought to establish rules that would set particular qualifications for congressional voting. They worried about what would occur if the Constitution offered as few restrictions as were contained in the Committee on Detail's draft. "Give the votes to people who have no property," Morris predicted, "and they will sell them to the rich." Madison expressed similar concerns. Foreseeing a time when "the great majority of the people" would be both landless and without "any other sort of property," Madison envisaged that popular majorities would either vote to enrich themselves at the expense of others or "become the tools of opulence and ambition," casting their votes to elect a plutocracy. In delegate John

Francis Mercer of Maryland's view, the cause for concern was more immediate. The people, he thought, "cannot know and judge of the characters of Candidates." For those who feared what mischief would result under the lenient provision in the draft constitution, the sensible solution was a stricter uniform rule.[57]

Ellsworth, on the other hand, believed that the nation's political marketplace should be monitored locally, not centrally through a restrictive constitutional mandate. As a result, he opposed proposals that would have removed the discretion of the states to set their own suffrage requirements. In his view, something positive was gained at the local level. State governments and local voters made better talent scouts than the federal government. "The states are the best judges of the circumstances and temper of their own people," he explained. It was not a mere matter of appeasing the public. On this matter, at least, wisdom was more likely to reside locally than nationally. The Philadelphia delegates were not in an ideal position to determine who among the American people, spread across thirteen states, should be eligible to vote in congressional elections.[58]

The question of whether congressmen—as opposed to congressional voters—should be required to hold property provided Ellsworth with still another opportunity to explain the rationale for electoral federalism. In reply to Charles Cotesworth Pinckney, the eloquent twenty-nine-year-old congressman and son of a wealthy South Carolina lawyer, who claimed that the property requirement would keep Congress in "independent and respectable hands," Ellsworth argued for delegating certain political decisions:

The different circumstances of different parts of the United States and the probable difference between the present and future circumstances of the whole, render it improper to have either uniform or fixed qualifications. Make them so high as to be useful in the Southern States, and they will be inapplicable to the Eastern States. Suit them to the latter, and they will serve no purpose to the former. In like manner what may be accommodated to the existing State of things among us, might be very inconvenient in some future state of them.[59]

The brief speech was almost as notable for what it did not say. Ellsworth never addressed the substance of Pinckney's point, namely that Congress would be more "independent and respectable" if legislative seats were limited to property owners. The primary question for Ellsworth was whether a constitutional mandate was the proper avenue for the proposed restriction. To answer this question, Ellsworth summarized the essential characteristics of a constitutional restriction. Such a measure would be uniform across the states and permanent until amended. Given what was entailed, Ellsworth counseled against the proposed property requirement. The motion to limit congressional office to property owners was dropped without a formal vote taken, so adamant was the delegates' opposition to it.[60]

During the Convention, Ellsworth also opposed what he regarded to be overly restrictive citizenship requirements for congressional membership. Under the draft constitution, foreign-born Americans could serve in the House of Representatives after three years of citizenship. Dismayed by the specter of "foreigners and adventurers mak[ing] laws for us," Virginia delegate George Mason moved on August 8 to boost the citizenship requirement to seven years. Ellsworth joined his fellow Connecticut delegates to cast their state's vote against Mason's measure. No other state joined Connecticut in maintaining the draft constitution's shorter citizenship requirement.

The following day, Gouverneur Morris took aim at the draft constitution's four-year citizenship requirement for senators. Citing the "danger of admitting strangers into our public counsels," Morris suggested adding ten years to the provision. Morris's fourteen-year rule appealed to delegates worried about letting those with "foreign attachments" into the legislative chamber responsible for approving treaties. Once again, Ellsworth and his Connecticut colleagues sought to protect the wide boundaries that the draft constitution had set for legislative membership, thereby ensuring that the range of electoral choices available to local voters would not be limited by a restrictive constitutional measure. Ellsworth claimed that Morris's measure would discourage "meritorious aliens from emigrating to this Country." The Connecticut delegation voted against Morris's proposed fourteen-year rule and the incrementally shorter proposals that followed, until a majority of the delegations—again with Connecticut opposing—agreed to the current nine-year citizenship requirement for senators.[61]

As with national citizenship, Ellsworth sought to fashion a residency rule that would leave local voters considerable leeway to determine the type of candidates that they wanted to represent them. On August 8, after Mason had successfully moved to extend the duration of citizenship required for congressional membership, John Rutledge of South Carolina proposed to limit the supply of congressional candidates to those who had resided for seven years in the state where they sought election. Rutledge defended his seven-year residency rule—which would apply to all office-seekers, native and foreign-born—on the ground that "an Emigrant from New England to South Carolina or Georgia would know little of its affairs and could not be supposed to acquire a thorough knowledge in less time." Ellsworth joined a chorus of delegates in opposition to Rutledge's measure. In place of Rutledge's seven-year requirement, Ellsworth moved for a constitutional requirement of only one year. Ultimately, the delegates decided that residency was not the proper benchmark, voting instead to require that congressional candidates inhabit the state they sought to represent. The move from residency to inhabitancy barred influential citizens from gaining congressional seats in states where they had established formal residency but in fact did not live. With this matter settled, Ellsworth formally moved to require one year of "previous inhabitancy" for congressional candidacy. On this matter, the delegates were willing to grant broad discretion to the states. The final constitutional provision required only that a congressional candidate be an inhabitant of the state "in which he shall be chosen" on the day of the election.[62]

In addition to favoring wide avenues for participation in congressional elections, Ellsworth supported several measures designed to extend the leverage of local voters by making electoral districts continuing sources of political power. Stating that it reflected the "fixed habit throughout our country," Ellsworth proposed annual elections for members of the House. A holdover from the Articles of Confederation, such a mechanism would keep congressmen on a short leash. Frequent election cycles encouraged representatives to return regularly to their home districts for necessary electioneering. Congressmen "ought to return home and mix with the people," Roger Sherman explained after Ellsworth raised a motion for annual elections on June 21. "By remaining at the seat of Government," added the elder Connecticut statesman, "they would acquire the habits of the place which might differ from those of their Constituents." But only Caleb Strong of Massachusetts and James Wilson spoke in favor of Ellsworth's motion, which never came to a vote.[63]

Ellsworth tried unsuccessfully to carry forward another feature of the Articles designed to make the nation's lawmakers more responsive to their constituents. The day after making his motion for annual congressional elections, Ellsworth proposed to permit the states to set salaries for congressmen elected within their borders. Hamilton excoriated the motion, predicting that it would turn Congress and state governments into rivals. But Ellsworth saw matters from a different perspective. "If we are so exceedingly jealous of state legislatures, will they not have reason to be equally jealous of us," he asked. "If I return to my home state and tell them, we made such and such regulations for a general government because we dared not trust you with any extensive powers, will they be satisfied? Nay, will they adopt your government? And let it ever be remembered, that without their approbation your government is nothing more than a rope of sand." By mid-August, however, Ellsworth reversed course. "In reflecting upon the subject," he told the delegates, he "had been satisfied that too much dependence on the states would be produced by this mode of payment." Ellsworth promptly motioned that congressional salaries be drawn from the central treasury. The delegates approved the proposal.[64]

In the debates surrounding the Connecticut Compromise, opponents of the equal state vote had accused Ellsworth of favoring a scheme that subverted majority rule. But as these other activities reveal, Ellsworth was distinct among the delegates for the extent to which he sought to involve the public in national politics, whether through annual elections or by allowing state lawmakers to fashion congressional membership and voter eligibility rules. By contrast, the same delegates who advocated popular apportionment in the Senate sought to limit the interaction between the American people and their government. As historian Gordon Wood notes, "to the Federalists"—a group whose ranks included Ellsworth's adversaries on apportionment, such as Madison, Hamilton, and Wilson—"the greatest dangers to republicanism were flowing not, as the old Whigs had thought, from the rulers or from any distinctive minority in the community, but from the widespread participation of the people in the government."[65]

The debates at the Convention demonstrated that proponents of popular apportionment were not interested in democracy for its own sake. Madison, Hamilton, and Wilson all merged support for popular apportionment with the notion that the existing Confederation granted the states too much power. The Articles, they argued, made it impossible to pursue the national interest. Their ultimate goal was to implement policies necessary for the peace and prosperity of the American nation, not to involve the public in national politics. Congress was to resemble Britain's Parliament, which Edmund Burke famously described as "a deliberative assembly of one nation, with one interest, that of the whole, where, not local purposes, not local prejudices ought to guide, but the general good, resulting from the general reason of the whole."[66] Popular apportionment, Madison, Hamilton, and Wilson contended, achieved this larger objective by removing the typically self-interested state governments from any formal role in the national political process.

Ellsworth's broader theory of representation presents a stark alternative to that of Alexander Hamilton—perhaps the most committed nationalist of the delegates. Hamilton argued at the Convention that the protection of the national interest required two steps: first, protect the national government from the states through popular apportionment; and second, protect the national government from the public itself. As in the case of the state governments, Hamilton made no secret of his fear of the people. The democratic spirit, he warned, was one of "amazing violence and turbulence."[67] Left to their own devices, popular majorities would clamor for unwise policies. "Take mankind as they are," he instructed the delegates, "and what are they governed by? Their passions."[68]

Permanency was Hamilton's solution to the problem of individual self-interest undermining the national interest. Beyond making the states, effectively, the subsidiaries of the national government, Hamilton proposed to install a quasicaste of life-tenured federal officeholders, permanent personnel immune to public pressure and therefore ideally positioned for the mission of pursuing the national interest. In particular, Hamilton sought to guarantee senators lifetime tenure in office. He claimed that the success of the British system resulted, in part, from the unelected nature of the House of Lords. "Having nothing to hope for by a change, and a sufficient interest by means of their property, in being faithful to the National interest, they form a permanent barrier against every pernicious innovation, whether attempted on the part of the Crown or of the Commons. No temporary Senate will have the firmness . . . to answer the purpose."[69] For the same reason, the New York delegate also proposed life tenure for the president. Once elected, an "Executive for life," Hamilton explained, would have no motive to sacrifice the national good for short-term political gain.[70]

Ellsworth, by contrast, favored local access to federal office-holders. Whereas Hamilton urged three-year terms for representatives (more frequent elections would create "too much dependence on the popular sentiments"), Ellsworth favored annual elections.[71] Whereas Hamilton desired to remove any financial influence that the states had over federal representatives (dismissing the low salaries that the states had typically paid to congressmen as "a bait to little demagogues"), Ellsworth proposed to fund the salaries of congressmen through local revenue streams.[72] Whereas Hamilton opposed granting state legislatures the power to choose senators, fearing that it would "vitiate" the Constitution, Ellsworth voted separately to make the state legislators the electors of senators.[73] Indeed, among the proponents of popular apportionment, only James Wilson wished to make the American people the electors of their senators.[74] The Virginia Plan gave this power to the House, while Hamilton would have the public choose electors for the purpose of selecting the permanent senators.[75]

Ellsworth seemed to want to replicate at the national level the harmony that he found in his home state. Along with other residents of Connecticut, he was proud of his state's history of self-government. At the time of the Convention, moreover, Connecticut remained a stronghold of Congregationalism. The political theology implanted by Connecticut's Congregationalists held that politics was of great importance. By registering their views in town meetings, the residents of Connecticut showed that they were chosen to live together in prosperity. The belief that politics was part of one's religious duty contributed to the acceptance of deliberative government inside and outside the Congregationalist churches.

Just as Connecticut's Congregationalist churches made use of elections to choose their ministers, the state's school committees chose their schoolmasters, enlisted militiamen their superior officers, and towns their deputies. These elections were frequent—no

Hamiltonian lifetime tenures for the Congregationalists. Connecticut's officials had to earn and re-earn the confidence of the state's residents. Elections for the state's General Assembly, for example, were held twice a year. Frequent elections operated, in the minds of many in Connecticut, as a necessary ingredient of republican self-government, a practice that kept both politicians and the electorate focused on protecting the public interest. In this way, the experience of his home state may have led Ellsworth to conclude that widening the avenues of political involvement could make for a more civic-minded public, one eager to show that it could distinguish between worthy and unworthy candidates, harmonious and divisive policies.[76]

Whatever its source, the success of Ellsworth's electoral federalism was no small matter. It ensured that the new government would be more attuned to the views of local constituencies in the formation of federal policy. In furnishing wide avenues for local participation, Ellsworth helped to keep American politics from becoming a theoretical science practiced by an isolated cadre of elites. It became, instead, a national sport where the actions of well-organized constituencies—for better or worse—frequently determined the score.

Slave Ties

During his final weeks in Philadelphia, Oliver Ellsworth helped protect another compromise. As with Senate apportionment, the Connecticut delegate insisted that his colleagues remember that their work still needed public approval. If their document demanded too much change, the entire project would be ruined. But this time, the fruits of Ellsworth's pragmatism were bitter.

Concerned that the reaction against any overly antislavery constitutional requirements would sink the new plan of government and leave the United States in political chaos, Ellsworth fought to ensure that the Constitution survived an eleventh-hour challenge to the document's proslavery provisions.

On August 8, two days after the Convention reconvened to consider the work of the Committee of Detail, North Carolina delegate Hugh Williamson moved to specify the precise formula for counting population for the purpose of congressional representation. Williamson's motion provided that House seats would be allotted according to the "rule hereafter to be provided for direction taxation," which held that such taxes would be "regulated by the whole Number of white and other free Citizens and Inhabitants . . . and three fifths of all other Persons."[77] In other words, Williamson proposed that representatives ought to be allotted to the states according to the combined number of free inhabitants and slaves that they possessed, only that the slave population would not be counted entirely but instead reduced to three-fifths of its total.

On its face, Williamson's proposal can be taken as an outright denial of the rights of enslaved African Americans to be counted as full members of the population. In fact, it was precisely in the interests of slave states to have their slave populations be counted entirely for the purpose of allotting representatives. Reckoning slaves in full meant that states with large slave populations would gain additional seats in Congress, as if the owned inhabitants of the various slave states were no different (despite the obvious fact that they were enslaved) from freemen. Thus the "three-fifths" formula to which Williamson alluded represented a compromise. While they could not count on additional representation in Congress for each slave held within their boundaries, the slave states would see their voting power in Congress increase by 60 percent of their respective slave populations.

Although Williamson's motion passed by a vote of nine states to two, the measure raised antislavery hackles. Massachusetts delegate Rufus King denounced the importation of slaves, noting that he could never tolerate an arrangement (then the case under the draft constitution) that permitted slaves to be imported with no future date given after which the practice would be abolished, while still allowing the slave states to gain additional seats for each slave carried or born within their boundaries. Gouverneur Morris was even more incensed, using the opportunity of the debate over the apportionment formula in Congress to decry slavery as "a nefarious institution" and "the curse of heaven on the states where it prevailed." In the midst of the antislavery rumblings, Roger Sherman attempted to calm the situation. Acknowledging that he too regarded the slave trade as "iniquitous," the conciliatory delegate nonetheless reminded the delegates that "the point of representation" had already been settled "after much difficulty and deliberation." Sherman's comment would not be the last time that he—or Ellsworth—would intervene to prevent the issue of slavery from harming the prospects of leaving Philadelphia with a constitution that would include the Connecticut Compromise.[78]

Two weeks after Williamson's apportionment motion, Maryland delegate Luther Martin challenged another provision protecting slavery. The drafting committee's constitution prohibited Congress from taxing the importation of slaves. Although King had made reference to it when he protested the three-fifths rule, until then this clause had not been discussed. Martin argued that the slave states gained too much under the document as it then stood. Not only would their congressional clout be enhanced as a result of the three-fifths rule, but they were also to receive a constitutional guarantee that the foreign slave trade would be tax free. Martin demanded that the slave states forfeit one of the above. He suggested allowing Congress to tax the importation of slaves in order to undo the "encouragement" that the three-fifths rule gave to slavery.[79] In response to Martin's motion, John Rutledge of South Carolina advised, "If the Northern States consult their interest, they will not oppose the increase of Slaves which will increase the commodities of which they will become the carriers."[80]

Succeeding Rutledge, Ellsworth voiced his support for protecting the slave trade from federal taxation. "Let every state import what it pleases," he stated. "The morality or wisdom of slavery are considerations belonging to the States themselves," which were "the best judges of their particular interest." Precedent dictated that the states should decide the legality of slavery. "The old confederation had not meddled with this point," and there was at present no "greater necessity for bringing it within the policy of the new one."[81]

The slavery debate resumed the following day, with George Mason stating the view that slavery and republican virtue could never be reconciled. "Every master of slaves," Mason explained, "is born a petty tyrant."[82] Ellsworth replied immediately. "As he had never owned a slave"—a thinly veiled shot at the Virginia delegate, who had brought with him to Philadelphia two of his more than three hundred bondsmen[83]—Ellsworth claimed that he "could not judge of the effects of slavery on character." Turning next to the subject at hand, Ellsworth provided another rationale for tolerating slavery. "Slavery in time," he predicted, "will not be a speck in our Country."[84] Ellsworth was likely relying, at least in part, on the general awareness that slavery had been under some political pressure since independence. Prior to the Convention, every southern state except Georgia enacted limits on the importation of African slaves during the period between the Revolutionary War and the Constitutional Convention.[85] In 1784, Ellsworth's home-state legislature had enacted the Gradual Abolition Act, which freed those henceforth born to Connecticut's enslaved population when they reached the age of twenty-five.[86] Given the possibility that the practice would somehow meet its ultimate demise in the not-so-distant future, Ellsworth advised his fellow delegates not to "intermeddle" with slavery.[87] But he was not finished. Once more he raised his voice to address the delegates, warning them this time that the present discord over slavery threatened the effort to frame a new plan of government. The delegates stood to "lose two States" if they failed to agree on the provisions now in place. Other states would remain "aloof" from the new government. The end result, Ellsworth solemnly admonished the framers, would be the rise of "several confederations and not without bloodshed."[88]

With the Convention threatening to dissolve over slavery on August 22, the delegates sent the matter to a special committee. Before the committee met, the eventual agreement was already in motion. The delegate who moved for the creation of the committee, Gouverneur Morris, proposed that it consider along with slave importation the provisions "relating to taxes on exports and to a navigation act." Morris predicted that "these things may form a bargain among the Northern and Southern states."[89]

According to historian Forrest McDonald, the deal had already been struck. Weeks earlier, at a private dinner party on June 30, Sherman had promised Rutledge that he would support South Carolina's interests in exporting its goods and importing slaves in return for Rutledge's protection of Connecticut's interest in a state-based Senate. After Rutledge delivered the votes for equal apportionment in the Senate, the Connecticut delegates worked to uphold their end of the bargain.[90]

Enter Ellsworth. While no evidence confirms that Ellsworth attended the Rutledge-Sherman dinner, weeks after the resulting South Carolina-Connecticut pact Ellsworth would serve with Rutledge on the Committee of Detail. The committee's draft afforded perpetual protection to the importation of slaves and required a two-thirds supermajority for navigation acts. Both provisions were critical to the interests of South Carolina and other exporting southern states. Navigation acts regulated the shipment of exports. At the time, northern states, in particular Massachusetts, dominated the shipping industry. The two-thirds requirement would prevent a simple sectional majority in the north from legislating a monopoly by freezing out foreign shippers from carrying southern exports.[91]

The debates over the drafting committee's report are additional evidence of Ellsworth's strenuous effort to keep intact the terms of the Sherman-Rutledge bargain. When Gouverneur Morris moved to lift the ban on export taxes, Ellsworth objected.[92] When the slave importation protection came under attack, Ellsworth stood alongside South Carolina's delegates.[93] When the two-thirds clause protecting exporters from navigation acts was challenged on the Convention floor, Ellsworth defended it.[94] The manner in which Ellsworth defended the several provisions that benefited southern states reveals that the Connecticut delegate believed that the draft constitution had struck a delicate balance. Ellsworth replied to Morris not simply to defend the prohibition of export taxes but also to warn the delegates against "deranging the order reported by the Committee."[95] When Morris later moved to send the matters of slave importation, the ban on export taxes, and the navigation act to a special committee, Ellsworth remarked that he favored "the plan as it is."[96]

Whether or not Ellsworth defended the draft constitution because of a Connecticut–South Carolina pact (historian Christopher Collier notes that no documentation apart from a Rutledge biography confirms that an explicit deal was struck between Rutledge and Sherman), one thing is clear.[97] Connecticut stood to gain much and lose little from the plan taking shape in the Convention. This alone may have been sufficient for Ellsworth and Sherman to resist any efforts to derail the momentum toward a final agreement along the lines of the drafting committee's proposal. Following the Connecticut Compromise, Ellsworth's home state had secured itself equal representation in the Senate, which ensured the state's role in the exercise of the federal government's powers. In barring states from laying impost taxes, the plan would free Connecticut's residents from continuing to pay taxes to the state of New York for goods imported through its ports. The ban on export taxes also helped Connecticut market its agricultural produce to its overseas, namely West Indian, trading partners.

Ellsworth's pragmatic approach toward slavery is further revealed in a letter dated March 7, 1790, and located in his personal papers. The correspondence indicates that Ellsworth was once approached to purchase a slave. The letter is addressed from New York, where Ellsworth had arrived to take his seat as a senator from Connecticut in the First Congress. It is a reply to correspondence that he had received from his wife, Abigail. It is apparent from Ellsworth's letter that he and Abigail had previously discussed a female slave who belonged to an officer known as Colonel Pattem.

After offering his greetings, Ellsworth resumes the relevant conversation in the letter's second full paragraph. "As to the negro girl," he writes, "I came to no agreement with Col. Pattem about her. In the little conversation we had I told him I should not take her as a slave for life but to hold only til she should be 25 years of age, which he seemed to approve of." Ellsworth's indication that he would hold the slave only until the age of twenty-five perhaps indicates that she was born after the enactment of the Gradual Abolition Act, which emancipated at this age all slaves born after March 1, 1784; or, as William R. Casto concluded in his Ellsworth biography, perhaps she was born before the law's enactment but Ellsworth was unwilling to hold her for life.[98]

In any case, Ellsworth reported that the colonel demanded "some purchase money" for the female slave. While he emphasized that ten pounds was the most that he was willing to spend, Oliver left the matter to Abigail, who appeared by the text of Ellsworth's letter to be the one in closer contact with Colonel Pattem. Since it was likely that the slave would cost less than ten pounds, Ellsworth gave Abigail permission to conclude the transaction. "You must act your own Judgment in the whole matter," he closed the letter, "and I shall be quite satisfied."[99]

As delegate in Philadelphia, Ellsworth had left the "wisdom or morality" of slavery to the states. Now he was deferring to his wife as to whether they would acquire a slave for a period of perhaps twenty years. The letter alone, however, does not indicate that either of the Ellsworths supported slavery. In a 1787 essay, Oliver expressed his belief that "all good men wish the entire abolition of slavery."[100] It may have been instead that Abigail was genuinely interested in helping a young and possibly orphaned child, who may otherwise have been sold into a lifetime of slavery in another state. For Ellsworth to condone the purchase of the young girl on those terms would be characteristic of his willingness to recommend a course of action designed to avoid a greater harm. According to the 1790 census, taken after Oliver's correspondence with Abigail, Ellsworth's household included one nonwhite free person, and no slaves. This accounting supports the conclusion that Oliver and Abigail decided to purchase the colonel's slave but then maintain her as an emancipated servant.[101]

On August 23, Ellsworth made his last floor speech before departing to Connecticut. The most likely explanation is that he felt impelled to tend to his duties behind the state bench.[102] Following Ellsworth's departure, the delegates reached a final resolution on slavery. They safeguarded the importation of slaves until 1808, when Congress was granted the power to ban the practice (which it did upon the lifting of the constitutional ban). In a related blow to slaveholding export states, the two-thirds requirement for the passage of navigation acts was also removed. But the slaveholding states could rest assured that despite the outcry from various delegates, the Constitution did not directly challenge the institution. Ellsworth's eagerness in quelling the potential revolt over slavery reveals the price that he was willing to pay to avoid the disorder that he feared would result from leaving Philadelphia without a plan of government, or with one that would not be ratified. For the onetime student of New Divinity Calvinism, the toleration of slavery was the unfortunate cost of national harmony.

Federalist Flourish

Because he departed the conclave in late August, three weeks prior to adjournment, Ellsworth was not present to affix his signature to the final document presented to Congress. While the Constitution does not bear Ellsworth's name, his influence can be seen in features from the equal state vote in the Senate and the localized federal election process to the Constitution's treatment of slavery.

It is an appropriate tribute to Ellsworth's balanced approach that he earned the esteem of both John C. Calhoun and Daniel Webster, nineteenth-century champions of states' rights and national unity, respectively. In 1847, Senator Calhoun hailed Ellsworth for the Connecticut delegate's opposition to the adoption of a national government that essentially would have abolished the states. In a speech on the Senate floor, the Connecticut-educated South Carolinian explained that "in the early stages of the convention there was a majority in favor of a national Government." "It is owing mainly to the States of Connecticut and New Jersey," he continued,

> that we have a federal instead of a national Government—that we have the best Government instead of the most despotic and intolerable on the earth. Who were the men of these States to whom we are indebted for this admirable Government? I will name them. Their names ought to be written on brass and live forever. They were Chief Justice Ellsworth, Roger Sherman, and Judge Paterson of New Jersey. The other States further South were blind; they did not see the future. But to the sagacity and coolness of these three men, aided by a few others, but not so prominent, we owe the present constitution.[103]

Calhoun's summation failed to mention that Ellsworth was also a majoritarian who never argued that a state deserved a constitutional right to resist a law that passed both houses of Congress. The Connecticut delegate's view of state power was practical, not doctrinaire. Thus Ellsworth argued only that the states be authorized to participate equally in the formation of federal policy and not that they should have the power to veto its enactment or disrupt its execution.

In 1833, Calhoun's counterpart Daniel Webster made exactly this point when, after referencing Ellsworth by name, the Massachusetts senator read directly from Ellsworth's defense of the Constitution at Connecticut's ratifying convention. "In republics," remarked Webster, quoting Ellsworth,

> it is a fundamental principle, that the majority govern, and that the minority comply with the general voice. How contrary, then, to republican principles, how humiliating, is our present situation. A single State can rise up, and put a veto upon the most important public measures. We have seen this actually take place; a single State has controlled the general voice of the Union; a minority, a very small minority, has governed us. So far is this from being consistent with republican principles, that it is, in effect, the worst species of monarchy.[104]

When Ellsworth's son William was a member of Congress, Webster confided to him that Oliver Ellsworth was the primary source of Webster's staunch opposition to the notion that a single state could nullify federal law.[105]

But Ellsworth would not have to wait a generation to notice his own influence. In addition to the constitutional provisions that may be traced to his efforts, the Connecticut delegate is also responsible for the way that Americans have long referred to their government. At the Convention, Ellsworth moved successfully to "drop the word *national*" as descriptive of any of the branches of the government set forth in the proposed constitution. Ellsworth requested that the new government be known as the government "of the United States." His colleagues unanimously agreed. To this day, Americans speak of federal, not national, programs, courts, and troops.[106] In the immediate wake of the Philadelphia Convention, the champions of the Constitution would call themselves *Federalists*. The term was particularly fitting for Ellsworth. As a constitutional delegate, he had successfully labored for a government that was federal in more than name only.

CHAPTER FOUR

"LANDHOLDER"

If there be any capital defects in this constitution, it is most probable that experience alone will discover them.

—Oliver Ellsworth, "Landholder V," December 3, 1787

"A Complete Master of the Subject"

The signing of the Constitution on September 17, 1787, ended one debate and began another. Although Oliver Ellsworth and his fellow delegates had emerged from Philadelphia with a new plan of government, they agreed that the Constitution would not become effective until nine of the thirteen states adopted it. The dynamic of the ratification debate would be different. For one, it brought the Constitution and its proponents into the public eye. Although there was some communication between delegates, ratification was a more decentralized process than the framing of the Constitution had been. For the former, the delegates gathered in one place; for the latter, they dispersed to their respective states.

Following the Convention, several of the framers, including Ellsworth, authored pro-Constitution newspaper essays. In keeping with contemporary practice, the widely circulated tracts were published pseudonymously. (Likewise, Alexander Hamilton and James Madison combined forces with John Jay, who was not a delegate, under the pseudonym "Publius" to publish their now famous *Federalist* essays prior to taking center stage at the New York and Virginia ratification conventions, respectively.) But the identity of the Constitution's defenders would not be concealed for long. In Ellsworth's case, his pro-Constitution essays were a precursor to his arguments at Connecticut's ratification convention, in which he appeared directly before his fellow citizens to defend the handiwork of Philadelphia.

As instructed by the state's General Assembly, Connecticut's ratifying convention gathered in the State House in Hartford on the first Thursday of 1788. Ellsworth was elected to represent Windsor at the convention. He would play a large role. Proponents of ratification chose Ellsworth to offer their opening address. (No record remains of the selection process). Three days later, Ellsworth returned to the convention floor to defend Congress's taxing power under the Constitution. Both times, his listeners were impressed. Describing Ellsworth's performance at the convention, Hartford attorney Enoch Perkins, who was on hand for the proceedings, remarked that Ellsworth had been "a complete master of the subject . . . armed on all points." Pierpont Edwards, who spoke before Ellsworth offered his address on the new government's fiscal powers, commented that when Ellsworth finished, so much illumination had been brought to the subject that Edwards "felt like a lightening bug in broad daylight."[1] Ellsworth's two recorded speeches (the only of perhaps several convention speeches of his that have been preserved) display the framer's deep understanding of the Constitution as well as his ability to simplify a potentially complicated case in such a way that his audience was convinced that there was only one correct decision. At the end of the convention, Connecticut became the fifth state to ratify the Constitution, by a lopsided vote of 128 to 40.

"The Honesty and Patriotism of the Gentlemen . . ."

The apparent irony of Ellsworth's skilled defense of the Constitution at the Connecticut ratifying convention is that he had been a vocal critic of holding ratification conventions in the first place. During the Constitutional Convention, the Connecticut delegate proposed that the Constitution be referred to the state legislatures—as opposed to popular conventions—for approval.[2] Ellsworth saw a great danger in the method that his colleagues ultimately adopted. With characteristic directness, he warned that popular conventions "were better fitted to pull down than to build up Constitutions."[3]

Ellsworth's grim portrayal of popular conventions was likely influenced by a bitter experience close to home. Four years earlier, several Connecticut towns, protesting a plan by Congress to provide former Continental Army officers with lifetime pensions, organized "a general convention" in the town of Middletown. Connecticut's political elite roundly denounced the gathering as an illegitimate and dangerous alternative to the state's well-established system of orderly government. Among their resolutions, the conventioneers drafted a slate of candidates to replace the state's pro-Congress lawmakers. Ellsworth, who was then bidding for a seat in state office, was among the targeted officials. Although Ellsworth survived the election contest, memories of Middletown may have convinced him that popular conventions were best avoided.[4]

Whatever his personal views on the matter, Ellsworth dealt with the acceptance of popular conventions as a successful lawyer might handle a defeat at a preliminary hearing. Without hesitation, Ellsworth adopted an argument that he had only recently opposed to obtain the verdict that he desired. In the first of a series of thirteen pro-Constitution newspaper articles, all signed "A Landholder" (most likely to emphasize that the anonymous author was a Federalist without guile, not a cosmopolitan merchant who sought a new government for the sake of his pocketbook), Ellsworth praised the decision to send the Constitution to the public for ratification. "It proves the honesty and patriotism of the gentlemen who composed the general Convention," he wrote in an essay that appeared in the November 5, 1787, edition of the *Connecticut Courant*, "that they chose to submit their system to the people rather than the legislatures, whose decisions are often influenced by men in the higher departments of governments, who have provided well for themselves and dread any change least [*sic*] they should be injured by its operation."[5] (All thirteen of Ellsworth's "Landholder" essays were published simultaneously in Hartford's *Connecticut Courant* and Litchfield's *American Mercury*).

Ellsworth was not the only framer who now defended what he had once opposed. Although Madison had pushed for a national government at the Convention, he had no qualms championing the fact that the plan of government would be "partly national" and "partly federal," the exact phrase that Ellsworth had used in opposition to the proposal to apportion Senate seats by population, as Madison and others wanted. That the Convention had been closed certainly made it easier for supporters of the Constitution to favor provisions that they once attacked. At least for Ellsworth, however, the move from framer to Federalist, from delegate to defender of the Constitution, did not require a great shift. He would have most likely agreed with the assessment of the twentieth-century historian Forrest McDonald, who wrote that the Constitution represented "a form of government more peculiarly adapted to the nature of the human animal than anything devised before or since."[6] Put simply, Ellsworth was proud of the framers' work. During the ensuing debate over ratification, he explained precisely why.

"United, We Are Strong"

In his opening address at Connecticut's ratifying convention, Ellsworth stated that the Constitution was "designed to supply the defects of the former system."[7] From Ellsworth's vantage, what occurred in Philadelphia was no revolution. Although it created a new government that would include two new branches and be equipped with a series of powers that had been heretofore exercised by the states, the Constitution, he contended, promised in substance only to complete the existing government.

But what was lacking in the Articles of Confederation was, for Ellsworth, nothing trivial. The federal government in its present form was failing to defend the American people. Accordingly, Ellsworth believed that the Constitution had a straightforward purpose and that the need for the Constitution was easy to identify and all but impossible to deny. "Mr. President," Ellsworth confidently began his opening remarks at Connecticut's ratification convention, "it is observable that there is no preface to the proposed Constitution; but it evidently presupposes two things: one is the necessity of a federal government; the other is the inefficacy of the old Articles of Confederation." Never one to tarry before a sitting jury, Ellsworth raised his main argument for ratification in exactly the next sentence. "A union," he continued, "is necessary for the purposes of a national defense. United, we are strong; divided, we are weak."[8]

A considerable portion of Ellsworth's defense of the Constitution revolved around what was then a simple point. To use a modern phrase, Ellsworth asked his audiences to ask themselves whether they felt safer now than four years ago—or, in this case, since the end of the Revolutionary War. To Ellsworth, the answer to this question was clearly no. America was experiencing a national humiliation, and still worse treatment was soon to come. The cause of it all was the principal defect of the Articles. The nation had no power, militarily or otherwise.

In his ratification speeches and essays, Ellsworth described the nation's current malaise. A chief cause was the fact that eighteenth-century America did not have two oceans to protect it from foreign powers. "Half a dozen regiments from Canada or New-Spain," wrote Ellsworth in a "Landholder" essay published on December 3, 1787, "might lay whole provinces under contribution, while we were disputing who has power to pay and raise an army."[9] As he explained during his opening address at Connecticut's ratification convention, the Confederation's inability to enforce foreign treaties endangered the citizens of the several states. Because certain states refused to comply with the treaty ending the Revolutionary War, stated Ellsworth, "Britain charges us with the breach, and refuses to deliver up the forts on our northern quarter."[10] From Ellsworth's view, Americans faced the specter of upheaval from homegrown forces. He wrote in "Landholder V," referring to Captain Daniel Shays, the Revolutionary War officer who was among the leaders of a popular uprising that compelled the state's governor to turn to private donors to muster an opposing force when it became clear that the Confederation government could not assist, "Had Shays, the malcontent of Massachusetts, been a man of genius, fortune and address, he might have conquered that state, and by the aid of a little sedition in the other states, and an army proud by victory, become the monarch and tyrant of America."[11]

Additionally, Ellsworth made clear that a powerless national government was also hurting Americans in their pocketbooks. Because the Confederation government posed no threat to them, foreign mercantile powers subjected Americans to merciless trading terms. Ellsworth emphasized that even modest American farmers were suffering as a result. "It may be assumed as a fixed truth that the prosperity and riches of the farmer must depend on the prosperity, and good national regulation of trade," he stated at the onset of his first "Landholder" essay. "Artful men may insinuate the contrary . . . ," Ellsworth continued, emphasizing the natural harmony between farmers and merchants,

> and excite your jealousy against the merchant because his business leads him to wear a gayer coat, than your economy directs. But let your own experience refute such insinuations. Your property and riches depend on a ready demand and generous price for the produce you can annually spare. When and where do you find this? Is it not where trade flourishes, and when the merchant can freely export the produce of the country to such parts of the world as will bring the richest return?[12]

But the economic harm caused by the Confederation, Ellsworth hastened to add, was in no way isolated from his larger point about the Confederation's military insecurity. An impoverished America would be easier to defeat. "Other nations," he warned in

"Landholder I," "will be pleased with your poverty; they know the advantage of commanding trade, and carrying in their own bottoms. By these means they can govern prices and breed up a hardy race of seamen, to man their ships of war when they wish again to conquer you by arms."[13]

Ellsworth did not approach the task of defending the Constitution principally as an academic exercise. He managed to reach into an emotion shared by Americans of his time or any time. Government's first responsibility is to defend its citizens. The conclusion of Ellsworth's opening address at Connecticut's ratifying convention exemplifies the emotional force that the Connecticut framer put behind his case for the new plan of government.

> Will our weakness induce the British to give up the northern posts? If a war breaks out, and a situation invites our enemies to make war, how are we to defend ourselves? Has government the means to enlist a man or buy an ox? Or shall we rally the remainder of our old army? The European nations I believe to be not friendly to us. They were pleased to see us disconnected from Great Britain; they are pleased to see us disunited among ourselves. If we continue so, how easy it is for them to canton us out among them, as they did the kingdom of Poland! But supposing this is not done, if we suffer the union to expire, the least that may be expected is that the European powers will form alliances, some with one state and some with another, and play the states off one another, and that we shall be involved in all the labyrinths of European politics.[14]

The message was powerful, no doubt, but Ellsworth's optimism that Connecticut would make what he considered to be the obvious choice measured his tone. "I do not wish to continue the painful recital," he closed. "Enough has been said to show that a power in the general government to enforce the decrees of the Union is absolutely necessary."[15]

"THE SWORD WITHOUT THE PURSE IS OF NO EFFECT"

The next step for Ellsworth was demonstrating that the Constitution was designed to protect the national interest in defense, foreign trade, and sectional harmony. It was one thing to point out that the Confederation was defective; it was quite another to demonstrate that the Constitution's cure was not worse than the Confederation's illness.

In his second address to Connecticut's ratification convention, Ellsworth took up the matter of the federal government's taxing power. Under the Constitution, Congress would have the power "to lay and collect Taxes, Duties, Imposts and Excises, to pay the Debts and provide for the common Defence and general Welfare of the United States." Characteristically, Ellsworth linked the taxing power to the need for a national defense, once again dealing with a potentially divisive issue (Congress's power to tax) by relating it back to the less controversial desire for national defense. And once again, Ellsworth's rhetoric was punchy, geared more for convincing his fellow delegates through succinct slogans than abstract theorizing. "Wars have now become rather wars of the purse than of the sword," he argued on the convention floor. "Government must therefore be able to command the whole power of the purse; otherwise a hostile nation may look into our Constitution, see what resources are in the power of government, and calculate to go a little beyond us." "For the sword without the purse is of no effect," he added in another memorable turn of phrase. "It is a sword in a scabbard."[16]

In treating both the power to tax and the power "to raise and support Armies," Ellsworth made a concerted attempt to appeal to those concerned that the Constitution moved too far in the direction of centralization. Federalists elsewhere were not so diplomatic—and their heavy-handed treatment of their opponents likely hampered the overall effort to gain popular support for a government manifestly "of the People." At one telling moment during Pennsylvania's ratification debate, James Wilson, who had battled Ellsworth over the equal state vote in the Senate, rose to his feet to interrupt Anti-Federalist William Findley. Findley's error, according to Wilson, lay in asserting that the country of Sweden gave up political liberty precisely when it abandoned jury trials. Since the Constitution explicitly granted no right to a jury trial, Findley's point was obvious. Only Wilson claimed that nothing of the sort had transpired in Sweden, and he dared Findley to prove it. It would take a few days to resolve the matter since the Wilson-Findley exchange soon gave way to a still more riotous taunting match between the dueling camps of delegates. Finally, adjournment was called. When the convention reopened several days later, Findley appeared with evidence in hand from William Blackstone's authoritative *Commentaries on the Laws of England*. Undeterred, Wilson used the lesson as an opportunity to put down Findley once again. "Those whose stock of knowledge," noted Wilson, "is limited to a few items may easily remember and refer to them," adding for good measure, "Young man, I have forgotten more law than ever you learned." Pennsylvania's ratification convention—the first to convene—seemed to offer Federalists a lesson in how not to proceed. It was indeed possible for Federalists to prevail in argument yet still fail. For the debate transcended the many dis-agreements over specific constitutional provisions. As Tocqueville wisely remarked of the French Revolution, "not mechanical legal structures but the ideas and the passions of men are the motive forces of human affairs." If the sentiments of the American people turned against the work of the framers, not even ratification would lead to a governable union.[17]

On the sensitive matter of taxes, Ellsworth correctly predicted that the early Congresses would collect the vast majority of federal revenues through a tariff on imported goods. (The national impost was responsible for more than 90 percent of federal revenue dur-ing the Washington administration).[18] This method of collecting taxes, Ellsworth remarked in his second ratification address, "will interfere less with the internal police of the states than any other species of taxation." The collection of federal taxes would then be, in Ellsworth's crisp phrasing, "chiefly a water operation." The fed-eral impost would replace the system which permitted port states to collect imposts on the goods that happened to travel through their borders to other states, keeping for themselves revenue that would now go to the general welfare and common defense of the nation. "If we do not give [the power to lay imposts] to Congress, the individual states will have it," stated Ellsworth. "It will give some states an opportunity of oppressing others, and destroy all harmony between them."[19]

Similarly, by creating a more efficient system for defending the nation, Ellsworth argued that the Constitution would prevent the need for far costlier military and political investments by the states. "Small states have enemies as well as great ones," remarked Ellsworth in his opening ratification address. "They must provide for their defense. The expense of it, which would be moderate for a large kingdom, would be intolerable to a petty state."[20] True to form, Ellsworth insisted upon raising the practical, if unpleasant, realities of statecraft. What would prevent a foreign power from invading a sparsely populated state far from the Confederation's capital? Without a union, where would such a state turn to defend itself? These very questions Ellsworth would ask in a later "Landholder" essay written to the citizens of New Hampshire in the midst of the state's ratification debate. To persuade them, Ellsworth emphasized the danger surrounding them. "Trust not to any complaisance of those British provinces on your northern borders," he wrote. "When the hour for a permanent connection between the states is past, the teeth of the lion will again be made bare, and you must either be devoured, or become its jackal to hunt for prey in the other states."[21]

Under the Articles, the Confederation mustered its forces through the state governments, which had proven to be an unreliable source of soldiers. Assuming that the central government would be of no assistance, as was the case during Shays's Rebellion, a state seeking to protect itself could rely entirely on its own forces, potentially ridding itself of its able-bodied men in case of a serious attack, or enter into defensive alliances with other states or even foreign nations. The Constitution changed all this. But the way that the framers solved the problem, explained Ellsworth in "Landholder III," was by making the federal government "*capable* of controlling the whole, and bringing its force to a point."[22] In other words, the Constitution's solution was not to create a sprawling military establishment. "In our case there is no want of *resources*," Ellsworth continued in the same essay, "but a want of a civil *constitution* which may draw them out and point their force."[23] An effective way to protect the people lay in permitting the federal government the means to raise and support a supply of federal troops. The Constitution had a deterrent effect. The framers had made the American people safer without requiring them to pay for anything more than the ink on a ratified document.

"Take Cognizance Only of National Questions"

Of course, not all of the ratification debate, in Connecticut or elsewhere, was about defense and taxes, despite Ellsworth's best efforts to shift the battle to the political terrain that he most preferred. Anti-Federalist critics of the Constitution seized upon a variety of other provisions, critiquing the framers for proposing to authorize Congress to regulate interstate commerce, ratify treaties, and create federal courts, all without the consent of the states. The new plan of government was also assailed for lacking a Bill of Rights.

Beyond defending the Constitution as necessary to provide for a national defense, Ellsworth believed that the framers' plan would continue to permit the states to perform all the functions that rightfully belonged to them. This was Ellsworth's broader view of the framers' intent for their plan of government. He understood the Constitution as a Federalist document—that is, one which separated powers between two separate levels of government according to the characteristics of the particular power. As Ellsworth noted during his opening ratification speech, the weakness of the Confederation "shows us the necessity of combining our own force, and, as to national purposes, becoming one state." The Constitution, claimed Ellsworth, delegated to the federal government only those powers that related to "national purposes." All else remained in the hands of the state governments and the American people.

A single remark in "Landholder IV" effectively captures Ellsworth's federalist perspective. The Constitution, he wrote, promised "no alteration" to the state governments, which were to "remain identically the same as they are now."[24] As any critic could have pointed out, however, the power of the states was *not* the same as a result of Article 1, Section 10 of the Constitution, which forbade the states from laying duties on imports or exports, making treaties, or carrying out any of a variety of activities that previously they had not been constitutionally barred from performing. But Ellsworth was making a more fundamental point, which he developed further in his superb second ratification address when he demonstrated that there could be more than one political authority in place over the same territory. To illustrate this point, Ellsworth gave the example of the Continental Army, which had tried individuals in its own courts during the Revolutionary War even though the civilian courts of the separate states were still in operation. According to Ellsworth, the crucial step for realizing how different public authorities could operate within the same territory was to recognize that certain decisions properly belong to certain authorities and not to others. By granting the military courts the authority to try military cases, Congress had not infringed upon the rights of the states. The jurisdiction of the military courts extended *only* to the adjudication of military matters. Congress had given military courts no authority to enter into the province of the state courts over ordinary civilian cases, such as disputes over contracts or wills.[25]

The authority that Congress had granted to the military was properly exercised by the military, not the states. As a result of a congressional resolution punishing desertion from the military, Ellsworth recalled that "a man was tried, condemned, and hanged, in [Hartford]." The fact that the trial occurred in a military court, outside the purview of the state, was acceptable because, as Ellsworth explained, the defendant "belonged to the army; he was a proper subject of military law." Because the trial of desertion and other military offenses concerned the military operations of all the states, it was acceptable that Congress, representing all the states, "had complete legislative, judicial, and executive power" over such matters.[26]

Ellsworth analogized that the same process had taken place with the Constitution. The framers had defined "the extent of the powers of the general government," and in so doing they had left other matters in the hands of the states. In the same way that Congress, during the Revolutionary War, had created a separate jurisdiction for military concerns, the framers had established a separate government empowered to resolve national political concerns.[27] As Ellsworth saw it, the Constitution gave the federal government the authority over issues where the interest of the nation was concerned, such as the regulation of interstate commerce and national defense. The states never had authority to act in these areas, Ellsworth believed, so the states forfeited no power that they truly had possessed prior to the adoption of the Constitution. "Some powers are to be given into the hands of your federal representatives," he wrote, "but these powers are in their nature general, such as must be exercised by the whole or not at all, and such as are absolutely necessary; or your commerce, the price of your commodities, your riches and your safety, will be the sport of every foreign adventurer."[28] In the same way that recognition of the military's authority over certain matters did not interfere with the genuine sovereignty of the states—no one of which had the proper authority to resolve a military issue that concerned the defense of the entire continent—the states had lost no sovereignty with the creation of a federal power with the authority to enforce the people's will in the determination of national political concerns. Thus the proper balance between the state and federal governments was established.

In the letter that he coauthored with Roger Sherman on the occasion of the Constitution's transmission to their home state's assembly, Ellsworth offered another reason why the Constitution did not challenge the authority of the states, directly at least. In their joint dispatch, Ellsworth and Sherman wrote that the proposed "restraint on the states" in such matters as emitting bills of credit, authorizing nonmoney as legal tender, and impairing contracts through ex post facto laws were "thought necessary as a security to commerce, in which the interest of foreigners, as well as of the citizens of the states, may be affected."[29] Under this formulation, the purpose of the Constitution was not, primarily, to subtract power from the state governments in these areas. Were the Constitution concerned only with limiting the power of the state governments, it could have done so directly, without granting the national government the additional authority to regulate foreign and interstate commerce. As Ellsworth and Sherman explained, however, the objective of the Constitution was to provide certain powers to the central government. In certain cases, this provision could not be accomplished unless certain state powers were also constrained.

This rationale may come across as constitutional hairsplitting, but the larger issue that it reveals is important: namely, Ellsworth's conviction that the federal and state governments had distinct responsibilities. In debate at Philadelphia, he stated that "the National Government could not descend to the local objects on which [domestic happiness] depended. It could only embrace objects of a general nature."[30] Similarly, after the Convention, Ellsworth wrote that under the new plan of government, Congress was authorized to "take cognizance only of national questions and interests which in their very nature are general."[31] Because Ellsworth maintained that the national government and the states occupied separate political spaces, he held that an enhancement in the power of the federal government did not necessarily reduce the power of the states. Thus Ellsworth could argue that the framers entered the province of the states only in the course of aggregating certain national responsibilities where they belonged.

From Ellsworth's perspective, the fundamental focus of the Constitution was on the federal government, not the states. The federal government received the powers enumerated in the various sections of the Constitution. All other matters were left to the citizens of the separate states to decide. As Ellsworth commented in "Landholder VI," this explained why the framers had not attached a Bill of Rights to their plan of government. "*There is no declaration of any kind to preserve the liberty of the press, etc.*," wrote Ellsworth, before offering his response to this critique. "Nor is liberty of conscience, or of matrimony, or of burial of the dead," retorted "Landholder." "It is enough that congress have [*sic*] no power to prohibit either, and can have no temptation. This objection is answered in that the states have all the power originally, and congress have only what the states grant them."[32]

According to Ellsworth, the framers' unifying objective and critical achievement was to create a Constitution that afforded federal officials the powers they needed to protect the common interests of their constituents, the people of the several states. As he and Sherman summarized it in their joint dispatch, "some *additional* powers are vested in Congress, which was a principal object that the states had in view in appointing the Convention."[33] Under the Articles, the nation had been suffering from a "*want* of a power sufficiently concentrated to promote its good," he wrote in a "Landholder" essay of November 19, 1787.[34] Ordinary landholders were left to rely upon "a government that was *incapable* of protecting them," having "*no constitutional power*" to pay those who defended the nation.[35] "All the interests of navigation and commerce must be protected by the union or come to ruin," he wrote in another essay, "and in our present system where is the power to do it?"[36] The primary mission and accomplishment of the Constitution, therefore, was to fill the gaps that prevented the existing union from being able to act as one.

Does the Constitution, in fact, reflect Ellsworth's perspective? Several of its provisions bear out his characterization of the federal government's powers as general in their character. The commerce powers that the Constitution granted to Congress are one example. Congress received the power to form commercial treaties with foreign trading partners and to set tariffs on goods entering the United States from abroad. The states, meanwhile, were barred from exercising these powers either at all (in the case of commercial treaties) or without congressional approval (in the case of imposts). Ellsworth did not consider this to be a material alteration to the federal-state balance because, as he explained, "the regulation of trade ever was and will be a national matter." For a commercial treaty or tariff to regulate the national economy, all the states must implement the terms of the treaty or the tariff. Since the states, acting individually, were never capable of regulating the national economy, the Constitution caused them to forfeit nothing. Similarly, the power to raise revenue for the common defense, to borrow on the credit of the United States, to establish naturalization and bankruptcy laws that are uniform across the states, to generate the nation's money supply and protect it from counterfeiting, and to place the nation in a state of war—these were all responsibilities that the framers assigned to the federal government and that the individual states could not adequately exercise.[37]

Ellsworth was not the only supporter of ratification who believed that the Constitution empowered the federal government to act only where "general" issues were at stake, leaving intact the states' plenary authority over local matters. The late historian Lance Banning once noted that from the onset of the Constitutional Convention, James Madison was occupied "less with the necessity of redistributing responsibilities between the central government and states than with the inability of the existing central government to do the tasks that everyone admitted were its proper business. 'Positive' additions of authority were needed, [Madison's] earliest reflections ran, so that the powers of the general government would reach all cases in which 'uniformity is proper,' 'as in trade, etc. etc.'" That Madison, one of the Constitution's chief architects, did not view the constitutional project as dedicated to relocating power from the states to the federal level lends credence to Ellsworth's position that by granting it the tools to perform the duties that the American people already expected of it, the Constitution changed how the federal government would operate, not what it could do.[38]

Alexander Hamilton, who, as a Constitutional delegate had proposed that the state governments be "extinguished" in the hope of streamlining the exercise of national power, explained that authority was not concentrated entirely at the national level under the Constitution.[39] "The administration of private justice between the citizens of the same State," he wrote in *Federalist* 17, "the supervision of agriculture and of other concerns of a similar nature, all those things in short which are proper to be provided for by local legislation, can never be desirable cares of a general jurisdiction."[40] John Marshall, who as chief justice of the United States would author the decision in *Marbury v. Madison* (1803) holding that the Supreme Court had the power to declare a law unconstitutional, likewise reflected,

> The genius and character of the whole government seem to be, that its action is to be applied to all the external concerns of the nation, and to those internal concerns which affect the States generally; but not to those which are completely within a particular State, which do not affect other States, and with which it is not necessary to interfere, for the purpose of executing some of the general powers of the government.[41]

Beyond the Constitution's text and the stated views of the framers, history may provide the best proof that others held Ellsworth's understanding of Congress's enumerated powers. During the century that followed ratification, federal officials, as a rule, did not take their constitutionally enumerated powers as an invitation for entering the province of the states. "If the purpose of the Constitution was to create a powerful national government," concludes Max M. Edling in his insightful, recently published study of the Constitution, then the century that followed ratification "may be read as one of the great ironies of history." Throughout the nineteenth century, the ordering of American public life still occurred primarily through the actions taken and policies pursued by the separate state governments. "Contrary to what Federalists and Antifederalists alike had predicted," writes Edling, "the states continued to be the most important element in the federal structure." Yet this outcome is less of a surprise when one accounts for the influence of Ellsworth's belief that the federal government's enumerated powers were designed so that its future leaders would do only what the states themselves could not.[42]

"THE JUDICIAL DEPARTMENT
IS A CONSTITUTIONAL CHECK"

While Ellsworth believed that the Constitution had adequately identified national powers, he realized that the enumeration of those powers in the Constitution alone might not guarantee that federal and state officials would remain within their respective domains. In his second ratification address, Ellsworth deployed another cleverly crafted analogy to make his point. "Each legislature," noted Ellsworth, referring to the state and federal governments, "has its province; their limits may be distinguished." He continued by comparing the allocation of powers between the two levels of government to the creation of a single road with two lanes, one for the states and the other for the federal government. "The road is broad enough," Ellsworth concluded, "but if two men will jostle each other, the fault is not in the road." The Constitution was the well-constructed road. The travelers were the occasionally less deliberative political actors that would now use the road.[43]

Significantly, Ellsworth also dwelt upon the precise mechanism that the framers had created to protect the Constitution's system of enumerated powers. In fact, the framers had created a branch of government to maintain the rules of the constitutional road. He referred, of course, to the federal courts. Ellsworth, who was a sitting state judge when he was called to serve as a delegate to the Constitutional Convention, was unique among the founders in outlining the role that the federal judiciary might play in the new government.

For Ellsworth, the federal judiciary's role in the system of enumerated powers had two sides. One side enforced legitimate actions; the other side invalidated illegitimate ones. First, as Ellsworth explained in "Landholder V," federal courts were necessary to carry out in practice the legitimate functions of the federal government. "A legislative power," he wrote, "without a judicial and executive under their control, is in the nature of things a nullity."[44] In passing laws, legislatures created rights. But if there were no courts where individuals could bring claims based on a violation of their statutory rights, the rights enacted by the lawmakers would not be guaranteed.

This particular mission of the federal courts—the enforcement of national rights, which included the rights of citizens under the Constitution or federal statutes passed in accordance therewith as well as the legitimate powers of the national government under the same—also defined the court's jurisdiction. The Constitution extended the province of the federal courts to certain cases, among them disputes where one party claims a right under the Constitution, a federal statute, or treaty. Ellsworth denied, however, that the Constitution permitted the federal judiciary to reach beyond the boundaries that the framers set for the federal government and hear a case in which no national issue was at stake. The jurisdiction of the federal courts did *not* extend into the province of the states. "Their courts," he wrote of the federal tribunals, "are not to intermeddle with your internal policy, and will have cognizance only of those subjects which are placed under the control of a national legislature." In a separate "Landholder" essay, Ellsworth reiterated the point. The judicial power, he wrote, "extends only to objects and cases specified, and wherein the national peace or rights, or the harmony of the states is concerned."[45]

If federal tribunals were necessary to *enforce* the legitimate powers of the national government, Ellsworth said, they could also be used to *prevent* the federal government from exceeding the sphere that the Constitution had created for it. He maintained that if Congress passed a law exceeding its enumerated powers, the law would be "void," a legal nullity that would have no claim on the American people. Speaking before Connecticut's ratifying convention, Ellsworth explained,

> This Constitution defines the extent of the powers of the general government. If the general legislature should at any time overleap their limits, the judicial department is a constitutional check. If the United States go beyond their powers, if they make a law which the constitution does not authorize, it is void; and the judicial power, the national judges, who to secure their impartiality are to be made independent, will declare it to be void. On the other hand, if the states go beyond their limits, if they make a law which is a usurpation upon the general government, the law is void; and upright, independent judges will declare it to be so.[46]

Federal and state courts were, quite logically from Ellsworth's perspective, under no obligation to enforce illegitimate decrees. Furthermore, the Constitution authorized a formal process by which a federal court could declare a law to be void. Because they were empowered to decide "cases and controversies" that might challenge the propriety of a congressional resolution, the federal courts were also situated to rule that a supposed law was, in actuality, a legal nullity—an unconstitutional act. Federal courts were to be the gatekeepers of the constitutional harmony between the general and the state governments.

Ellsworth believed, moreover, that the framers designed the judiciary such that federal judges—as opposed to other members of the federal government—could be trusted to review federal laws. Federal judges, he wrote, were "made independent."[47] By this, Ellsworth did not mean that judges were free to exercise their own independent judgment as to the wisdom of a law. The role of the judicial department, as he explained at his state's convention, was to strike down actions by the national government that went "beyond their powers." Judicial independence came instead from the fact that federal judges were separate persons from the federal legislators and thus not the judges of their own laws. Additionally, judges were "made independent" under the Constitution by not having to face reelection. If the American people disliked federal courts for enforcing an unpopular law, their proper recourse was to elect new lawmakers.

By making the judiciary the arbiter of constitutional questions, the framers had carved out an important role for the public in limiting the federal government's powers. Federal judges were not the only individuals who had no obligation to enforce "void" laws. As the Supreme Court put it in *Calder v. Bull* (1798), "that *no man* should be compelled to do what the laws do not require" is "a fundamental principle" that "flows from the very nature of our free Republican governments."[48] The federal judiciary provided a venue wherein citizens could bring a challenge to a rights violation. And they did. In *Empire of Liberty*, his splendid history of the founding era, Gordon Wood comments that judicial review emerged in early America in part because the provisions of the Constitution could be "litigated in the ordinary court system." Writes Wood, "America's federal and state constitutions may be higher laws, special acts of the people in their sovereign capacity, but they are just like lowly legislative statutes in that they are implemented through the normal practice of adversarial justice in the regular courts."[49] If the electorate disagreed with the constitutional reasoning of a lawmaker, voters had a remedy at the ballot box. But that was not all. If a party's constitutional rights were violated, he could sue.

On the role of the federal judiciary, the true fault line between Anti-Federalists and Federalists lay in how each side predicted the new federal courts would rule. Contrary to later commentators who maintain that John Marshall invented judicial review from whole cloth in *Marbury v. Madison*, both the Constitution's leading supporters and opponents, who considered the question of judicial review, agreed that federal judicial review was in the Constitution. The Anti-Federalist critic "Brutus," for example, remarked in his "Letter No. XI," published on January 31, 1788, in advance of the New York ratification convention, that Article III, Section 2 of the Constitution, extending the power of the federal courts to cases concerning the federal statutory and constitutional law, "vests the judicial with a power to resolve all questions that may arise in any case on the construction of the constitution." And later in the same essay: "[the federal judiciary] will give the sense of every article of the constitution that may from time to time come before them." Noting that the Constitution authorized the federal judiciary to serve as "the last resort" in constitutional disputes, Brutus further explained, "It will not be denied that the constitution is the highest or supreme law. And the courts are vested with the supreme and uncontrollable power, to determine in all cases that come before them, what the constitution means. They cannot, therefore, execute a law, which in their judgment opposes the constitution, unless we suppose they can make a superior law give way to an inferior one."[50]

The Anti-Federalist Brutus doubted that the federal courts would require the other federal branches to adhere to the literal limits set by the Constitution's text. Federal judges, Brutus continued in his next missive, published on February 7, 1788, "will in their decisions extend the power of the government to all cases they possibly can, or otherwise they [i.e., the national government] will be restricted in doing what otherwise appears to be the intent of the constitution . . . to wit, pass laws and provide for the execution of them, for the general distribution of justice between man and man." Duly relying upon Blackstone as his source for the rules on statutory construction, Brutus maintained that a good judge will interpret a law in light of the lawgiver's intent. So even a good federal judge, Brutus predicted, would find himself upholding exercises of federal power.[51]

From the Anti-Federalist's view, the problem was not with judicial review—it was with the Constitution itself. The document plainly gave federal judges the power to settle constitutional questions. To Brutus, this was a mistake. In his final commentary on the issue dated March 20, 1788, Brutus suggested a more popular alternative to judicial review. He preferred making Congress the ultimate arbiter of constitutional conflicts. "Had the construction of the constitution been left to the legislature," he opined, "they would have explained it at their peril. . . . [I]f they determine contrary to the understanding of the people, an appeal would lie to the people at the moment when the rulers are to be elected." As the Anti-Federalist's readers now realized, however, the Constitution had not chosen Congress as, in Brutus's words, "the last resort" for "determin[ing] the sense of the compact." This was the job of the federal judiciary.[52]

The two principal authors of the *Federalist Papers*, Hamilton and Madison, agreed that the framers had designed the judiciary to serve as a constitutional check. Unlike Brutus, of course, the *Federalist* authors predicted, at least publicly, that the courts would enforce the framers' plan for a limited federal government. Constitutional limits on Congress's power, wrote Hamilton in *Federalist* 78, "can be preserved in practice no way other than through the medium of the courts of justice; whose duty it must be to declare all acts contrary to the manifest tenor of the constitution void." Federal judges were "the bulwarks of a limited constitution against legislative encroachments" and "an essential safe-guard against the effects of occasional ill humours in the society." Yet as Hamilton explained, this did not mean that federal judges were superior to members of the other federal branches. The judiciary's duty to strike down an unconstitutional statute came from the duty to follow the Constitution, a duty that bound all members of the federal government equally.

A constitution is in fact, and must be, regarded by the judges as a fundamental law. It therefore belongs to them to ascertain its meaning as well as the meaning of any particular act proceeding from the legislative body. If there should happen to be an irreconcilable variance between the two, that which has the superior obligation and validity ought of course to be preferred; or in other words, the constitution ought to be preferred to the statute, the intention of the people to the intention of their agents.

Although he did not address the subject in the *Federalist*, James Madison expressed the same view in his lengthy October 24, 1787, letter to Thomas Jefferson, in which he explained to his fellow Virginian, who had been serving as ambassador to France during the Convention, that the framers had authorized the federal judiciary to "declare [an unconstitutional law] void after it is passed.[53]

While Hamilton and Madison shared Ellsworth's view of the role of the federal courts under the Constitution, neither *Federalist* author was particularly enthused with the fact that the framers had opted to make the judiciary the constitutional check. Both believed that the federal judiciary represented perhaps the least intrusive constitutional check that the framers could have fashioned. It bears repeating that one of the views that placed Hamilton and Madison in the nationalist camp at the Convention was their distrust of state governments. A month prior to the Convention, Madison compiled a list of "The Vices of the Political System of the United States" (his title), many of which, in the author's opinion, had been committed by the state governments. The first item on the future delegate's list was the "Failure of the States to comply with the Constitutional requisitions," followed by "Encroachments by the States on the federal authority." The third item addressed the recent propensity of state governments to violate "the laws of nations and treaties." And so on. If anything, Hamilton's estimation of the state governments was even lower. "The States have constantly shewn a disposition rather to regain the powers delegated by them than to part with more, or to give effect to what they had parted with," he remarked at the Convention. "The ambition of their demagogues is known to hate the controul of the Genl. Government."[54]

Thus both Madison and Hamilton largely took for granted that encroachments on the Constitution would come from the states.

"What, for instance, would avail restrictions on the authority of the state legislatures," barred by the Constitution, for example, from coining money, passing laws impairing the obligations of contracts, as well as giving titles of nobility, "without some constitutional mode of enforcing the observance of them," asked Hamilton in *Federalist* 80.[55] In his post-Convention report to Jefferson, Madison expressed that "the representatives of Counties and Corporations in the Legislatures of the States [are] much more disposed" than federal officials "to sacrifice the aggregate interest, and even authority, to the local views of their constituents." Presuming that "the danger of encroachments" was "much greater" from the states, Madison reasoned that "the Judicial authority under our new system will keep the States within their proper limits, and supply the place of a negative on their laws."[56] Accordingly, as Constitutional Convention delegates, both Madison and Hamilton had proposed what they considered to be more powerful constitutional checks on the states. The Virginia Plan included a federal legislative veto of state acts, authorizing a majority in Congress to nullify any state law that, in the opinion of Congress, contravened the Constitution. Hamilton went even further. He sought to grant the federal government the power to prohibit state actions *prospectively*. "The better to prevent such laws from being passed," Hamilton proposed that state governors, appointed by the federal government, "shall have a negative upon the laws about to be passed" in their respective states.[57]

Both proposals promised to have a centralizing effect. A majority in Congress (in Madison's case) or a single federally appointed governor (in Hamilton's) would have had the power to nullify a state law. In contrast to Madison's and Hamilton's proposals, the veto tool that the framers created required individual litigants to take the initial steps necessary for enforcing their constitutional rights. The fact that the initiation of a constitutional check through the judiciary would have to bubble up through the courts, and not flow downstream from Congress, failed to satisfy Madison, who worried in his post-Convention missive to Jefferson that "individuals . . . may be unable to support an appeal against a State to the supreme Judiciary." Considering another practical point, Madison noted further that the congressional veto would likely take effect earlier than a judicial veto, which must come sometime after the unconstitutional act, all depending on when the case challenging the encroachment is decided. Echoing Hamilton's rationale for empowering state governors with the veto pen, Madison commented that it was "more convenient to prevent the passage of a law than to declare it void after it is passed."[58]

Hamilton's disappointment with the framers' constitutional check can be gleaned from the context of his *Federalist* essays on the subject. The entirety of Hamilton's treatment of the federal judiciary's powers is found in six successive essays, *Federalist* 78–83, which appeared at the very end of Hamilton's collection of proratification essays. Only two essays follow *Federalist* 83, one of which deals with miscellaneous objections, most significantly the lack of a Bill of Rights; the other contains the authors' closing remarks. Hamilton did not publish his judiciary essays until eight states had already ratified the Constitution. It is most likely that Hamilton wrote these essays in the first place more out of a feeling of necessity than desire. Someone had to reply to Brutus before the opening of the New York convention, scheduled for June 17, 1788. *Federalist* 78–83 all postdate March 20, 1788, the publication of Brutus's final assault on the judiciary.[59] Unlike all of the previous *Federalist* essays, which were first circulated in newspapers and shortly thereafter reprinted as a book (typically called the

M'Lean Edition after its publishers), Hamilton's judiciary essays were released only in the second volume of the M'Lean Edition, which collected *Federalist* 37–77 as well as the heretofore unpublished judiciary pieces and appeared in time for the New York convention.[60]

While *Federalist* 78 contains the most quoted line by Hamilton or perhaps any framer on the powers of the federal judiciary, this *Federalist* essay should be read alongside Hamilton's other judiciary essays published on the same date. Together, these six essays offer a fuller view of Hamilton's opinion on the federal judiciary. In particular, in *Federalist* 80 Hamilton partially reveals his own disillusionment with the framers' decision to lodge the constitutional check with the federal courts. The requirement to keep the states within their constitutionally stated limits, Hamilton writes, must be enforced through either "a direct negative on the state laws, or an authority in the federal courts." "The latter," he then concludes, "appears to have been thought by the convention preferable to the former, and I presume will be most agreeable to the states." Taken with Hamilton's vocal support of a national veto at the Convention, his tone in *Federalist* 80 indicates that the judicial veto was less than agreeable to him. For this reason, Hamilton's famous words from *Federalist* 78 that the judiciary was the "least dangerous" branch and "beyond comparison the weakest of the three departments of power" may be best understood not just as descriptions of the actual plan of government drafted in Philadelphia but also as further evidence of Hamilton's personal disappointment that the framers failed to adopt a more "dangerous" constitutional check.

On the question of judicial review, then, it can be concluded that Ellsworth accurately informed the delegates of Connecticut's ratification convention that, under the framers' plan, constitutional law would be enforced ultimately through federal courts. Ellsworth most likely believed that the framers had struck the correct balance. Unlike the *Federalist* authors, the Connecticut delegate never articulated any support for a more centralized enforcement power. Ellsworth was sensitive to the amount of constitutional change that the electorate was willing to tolerate. The framers had created a Congress with the ability to levy taxes and raise armies. It would be naïve to expect the states to ratify a plan of government that also included a congressional veto, not to mention Hamilton's proposal for federally appointed state governors authorized to do the same. As his crafting of the Judiciary Act of 1789, discussed in the next chapter, will show, Ellsworth believed that many cases involving federal law could be tried first in the state courts. Litigants in these cases would have to take the additional step of appealing their cases to a federal court before any such court would have the chance to assess the applicable federal statute or constitutional provision. Ellsworth's subsequent actions, in short, confirm that he was concerned with the potential political backlash were Congress to create an extensive system of federal courts. The Connecticut Federalist would further tame the "least dangerous branch."

"Perfection Is Not the Lot of Human Institutions"

Historians have included "Landholder" among the "other" Federalist writings, the label given to the broad survey of letters, articles, pamphlets, and published speeches that are not among those essays drafted chiefly by Madison and Hamilton and included in their famous collection. In part, the descriptive is meant to be dismissive. It alerts readers to the singular greatness of *The Federal-*

ist. And, no doubt, none of the "other" Federalists, whose ranks included James Wilson, John Dickinson, James Iredell, Roger Sherman, and Ellsworth, were able to sustain—or, in some cases, reach—the theoretical depth found in *The Federalist*. Putting aside the effectiveness of Ellsworth's proratification writings, it is certainly fair to place "Landholder" in the category of "other" Federalists. Given Ellsworth's practical orientation, it is unlikely that "Landholder" could have produced anything along the lines of the *Federalist's* broad and profound analysis. Regardless, that was not Ellsworth's goal. His effort was geared to a narrower, though still crucial, purpose: the ratification of the Constitution.[61]

Another important factor, however, contributes to the "otherness" of Ellsworth's proratification writings—their religious undertone. Throughout the ratification debate, the doctrines of New Divinity Calvinism informed Ellsworth's outlook. By contrast, the primary *Federalist* authors, Madison and Hamilton, were more influenced by patterns of thought that emerged from the Scottish Enlightenment, the mid-eighteenth-century flourishing of scientific, economic, and political insight whose contributors included David Hume, Francis Hutcheson, and Adam Smith. Hence Ellsworth's intellectual "otherness."

Indeed, it was not simply that Ellsworth believed that the Constitution was part of God's divine plan for the United States (though he did attribute the "unexpected harmony of the federal Convention" to "the special influence of heaven").[62] "Landholder's" former tutor, Reverend Joseph Bellamy, had taught that the "sight of the wisdom of God in the permission of sin, is very useful to promote holiness of heart and life."[63] Ellsworth accordingly saw the hand of God in the chaos of the Confederation. In "Landholder V," for example, he explained that even the most irresponsible protests (from Federalist eyes) against political centralization seen during the Confederation were ordained by God for the purpose of creating a groundswell of support in the opposite direction. Scared stiff by Shays's Rebellion and driven to a rage by the actions of Rhode Island—"Wrong Island," as then decried, was the bête noire of proponents of a stronger union since, among other things, the tiny state refused to amend the Articles to permit a federal impost—the American people would come to their senses. The prodigal states would return home. Such was God's design. "The little state of Rhode Island," wrote Ellsworth,

> was purposely left by Heaven to its present madness, for a general conviction in the other states, that such a system as is now proposed is our only preservation from ruin. . . . The rebellion of Shays and the present measures of Rhode Island ought to convince us that a national legislature, judiciary and executive, must be united, or the whole is but a name; and that we must have these, or soon be hewers of wood and drawers of water for all other people.[64]

So convinced was Ellsworth that God had tolerated the misdeeds of Rhode Island to spur support for a new union that he addressed an entire "Landholder" essay to the "Rhode Island Friends of Paper Money, Tender Acts, and Anti-federalism," explaining to his wayward northeastern neighbors that now was the time for them to mend their reckless ways. God's plan for them had come to pass. "The singular system of policy adopted by your state, no longer excites either the surprise or indignation of mankind," began the letter. "For this end Heaven permitted your apostasy from all the principles of good and just government," Ellsworth continued. "By your system we see unrighteousness in the essence, in effects, and in its native miseries. The rogues of every other state blush at the exhibition, and say you have betrayed them by carrying the matter too far. The very naming of your measures is a complete refutation of anti-federalism, paper money and tender acts, for no man chooses such company in argument."[65]

And yet putting aside the religious underpinnings of Ellsworth's proratification defense, what is remarkable is the degree to which Ellsworth and the more renowned *Federalist* authors reached the same conclusions. New Divinity Calvinism had shaped Ellsworth to believe that the different parts of society needed to work together in harmony to bring about God's plan. He waited no longer than his first "Landholder" essay to convince his readers that the division of society into farmers and merchants was not to be regretted. Rather, the prosperity of all was a consequence of the mutual cooperation of society's interconnected parts. "Your property and riches," he addressed his fellow "holders and tillers of land," "depend on a ready demand and generous price for the produce you can annually spare. When and where do you find this? Is it not where trade flourishes, and when the merchant can freely export the produce of the country to such parts of the world as will bring the richest return?"[66]

The underlying principle of the *Federalist* was no different. Contrary to the Anti-Federalist desire for a simpler society, with fewer outward distinctions among the citizenry, Publius championed the diversity of interests held by the American people. It may be said that the first *Federalist* essay was written in 1776—not Jefferson's splendid Declaration, but Adam Smith's *An Inquiry into the Nature and Causes of the Wealth of Nations*. For Smith, the "wealth of nations" was not their natural resources or anything material for that matter, but the capacity to cultivate and maintain a diverse economy. The material success of a nation depended precisely on what might be termed its "economic constitution." Smith explained: "It is the great multiplication of the productions of all the different arts, in consequence of the division of labor which occasions, in a well-governed society, that universal opulence which extends itself to the lowest ranks of society."[67]

Ellsworth and the *Federalist* authors viewed a stronger national government—or just *any* national government—as necessary to regulate America's diverse interests. In *Federalist* 10, Madison famously wrote that the size of the proposed union would prevent any single faction from dominating the new government. Rather, the federal government—the "large republic" that the framers had created—offered favorable conditions for the development of prudent public policies because the nation's various interests could be expected to moderate each other once they were collected at the national level according to the framers' plan. Madison's large republic, in short, did for politics what Smith's free marketplace did for economics. It provided the conditions under which the public would not be stuck with public policies that represented only the interest of the dominant or monopoly party.[68]

Once again, Ellsworth's approach turned out to be similar, though for "Landholder" the states were the principal entities whose diverse and often conflicting interests needed to be balanced. In *Federalist* 10, Madison had focused on economic and ideological groupings, listing, as examples of factions, the landed, manufacturing, mercantile, and moneyed interests. The factions that mattered to Ellsworth were established political communities. While *Federalist* 10 operated largely on a theoretical level, Ellsworth's claim that a stronger national government was necessary to prevent the individual states from exploiting each other made sense empirically. No matter how unenlightened it was for Americans to group themselves by states, the fact of the matter was that they did. And it was also true that states had real power, which, quite understandably from Ellsworth's perspective, needed to be checked. "If divided," he asked in his opening ratification address, "what is to prevent the large states from oppressing the small? What is to defend from the ambition and rapacity of New York, when she has spread over that vast territory which she claims and holds?" After all, it was an "incontrovertible fact," as he reminded the delegates in his second ratification address, that New York was lining its pockets with the taxes that it levied on Connecticut residents for the goods that traveled through New York's ports.[69]

Ellsworth's identification of the states as dangerous factions gave his proratification arguments a polemical quality, which probably only increased their effect. Naturally, few if any of the delegates at Connecticut's ratification convention would have been offended to hear that the government of New York, or any other state for that matter, was a significant cause of the nation's woes. Ellsworth's sensitivity to the actual, if not always enlightened, sentiments of his audiences was likely among the reasons why Rufus King believed that "the 'Landholder' will do more service" for the cause of ratification "than the elaborate works of Publius."[70]

Finally, Ellsworth's religious perspective also prevented him from presenting the Constitution as a utopian solution. Here again, the difference between Ellsworth's "otherness" and the more secular approach of the *Federalist* is not as stark as may be imagined. For one, the authors of the *Federalist* still took for granted the reality of human selfishness. As Madison wrote in *Federalist* 51, "If men were angels, no government would be necessary." On this point,

Ellsworth needed no convincing. For him, the Constitution was an improvement largely because it established the order necessary to check the most egregious and dangerous threats to the nation's political liberties. "Perfection," he reminded his readers, "is not the lot of human institutions." No plan of government, however well designed, could undo the effects of original sin. "When we become ignorant, vicious, idle," he warned in another essay, "our liberties will be lost—we shall be fitted for slavery, and it will be an easy business to reduce us to obey one or more tyrants."[71]

"Landholder" maintained that a lot depended on the American people and the officials that they elected to serve in the new government. Since his studies under Reverend Bellamy, Oliver Ellsworth understood that righteous leaders were necessary to discern God's plans for their fellow citizens. Since the Almighty had not stopped acting in this world, neither would Ellsworth. A year after his successful defense of the Constitution, this "other" Federalist would become a leading senator. It was now Ellsworth's turn to show that the nation's legislature could be trusted with the responsibility—in the words of "Landholder III"—"of controlling the whole, and bringing its force to a point."[72]

CHAPTER FIVE

COURT-MAKER

In forming this branch, our objects are—a fair and open, a wise and impartial administration of justice, between the public and individuals, and between man and man.

—"Federal Farmer," January 18, 1788

"A Bill for Organizing the Judiciary"

Following the ratification of the Constitution, Oliver Ellsworth was selected by Connecticut's legislature to serve in the inaugural class of the United States Senate. The new senator reported promptly to the federal capital in New York. "Most of the members from the Eastern States are arrived," Ellsworth wrote Abigail after completing the three-day journey from Hartford, "but not a sufficient number yet from the Southward to proceed to business." Although the Senate lacked the necessary number of lawmakers to open its doors officially, Ellsworth was not content with sitting idle. Now forty-four, and seasoned from his multiple national and state posts, the Connecticut senator seemed focused. In the weeks that he waited for the Senate to open its chambers, Ellsworth readied himself for legislative action, pondering perhaps how he could seize from the outset a leading role in the new Senate. "I employ my time as I presume a numbers of others do," he explained to Abigail, "in looking into & preparing for the business we are soon to enter upon."[1]

When a quorum of lawmakers finally assembled in April 1789, the Senate appointed its first committee, which was tasked with compiling "a bill for organizing the Judiciary of the United States." Because the proceedings of the First Senate were closed to the public, it is uncertain whether Ellsworth was responsible for pushing the creation of federal courts to the top of the chamber's legislative agenda. However, it would be plausible if Ellsworth, a former state judge, prompted his colleagues to focus their attention first on establishing a national system of courts. The available records from the inaugural Senate's proceedings and the correspondence of the senators do make clear that Ellsworth directed the enactment of the historic Judiciary Act of 1789. The bill, Ellsworth's most significant legislative accomplishment during his seven years in the U.S. Senate, has the essential marks of the New Divinity–trained Connecticut senator's consensus-driven moderate Federalism.

"The Sore Part of the Constitution"

In the summer of 1787, supporters of a stronger central government at the Constitutional Convention prevailed on a crucial point. The federal government, they convinced their fellow delegates, needed its own courts. The opposing point of view was expressed by John Rutledge early on in the proceedings when the influential South Carolina delegate declared that he was against "establishing any national tribunal except a single supreme one." Rutledge was immediately seconded by Roger Sherman of Connecticut, Ellsworth's political mentor. According to James Madison's notes, Sherman, an eighteenth-century fiscal conservative, "dwelt chiefly on the supposed expensiveness of having a new set of Courts, when the existing State Courts would answer the same purpose."[2]

The delegates, in short, had no trouble creating a Supreme Court, but they were split over the proper number of lower federal courts. As with other matters, the rival camps reached a compromise. Those who hoped that Congress would make use of the state courts prevented their colleagues from creating any "inferior tribunals." But supporters of a larger federal judiciary also secured an important victory. Congress gained the authority to create lower federal courts. The precise language of the constitutional compromise supplied the federal government with "one Supreme Court" as well as "such Inferior Courts as Congress may from time to time ordain and establish."

Less constitutional ink meant more congressional power. The fewer words the framers used to set forth a congressional power, the fewer the restrictions, provisos, and conditions contained therein. With respect to creating lower federal courts, the framers' approach was short and thus sweet for proponents of congressional authority. Article III of the Constitution provided one substantial limit to Congress's discretion, restricting the federal government's judicial power to certain matters in which there was a particular federal interest, such as suits where the U.S. government was a party, suits between states or between citizens of different states, and cases involving federal statutes, treaties, or constitutional provisions. The Constitution did not, however, automatically give the federal courts the power to hear these kinds of disputes—it simply provided that nothing else could be heard in the federal judicial system. Instead, the framers authorized Congress to determine which, if any, of these matters could be filed in federal courts and which would have to be heard in state trial courts.

This was no small matter. Many of the nation's early leaders were opposed to relying on the states to enforce congressional resolutions. At the Constitutional Convention, James Madison summarized the Federalist case for federal courts: "A Government without a proper Executive & Judiciary would be the mere trunk of a body without arms or legs to act or move."[3] Article VI of the Constitution—establishing the supremacy of federal law and requiring state judges to swear to support the Constitution— was, by itself, insufficient. So was the appellate review power of the U.S. Supreme Court. To Federalists, at least some federal trial and appellate courts (in addition to the U.S. Supreme Court) were needed if federal interests were to be adequately protected. But to Anti-Federalists, federal courts sounded dangerously similar to the British tribunals that had brought Parliament's demands to bear on the American colonists. As Edmund Pendleton, a prominent Virginia judge and shrewd observer of national politics, wrote at the time, the federal judiciary was "the Sore part of the Constitution & requires the lenient touch of Congress."[4]

A Congenial Subcommittee

Americans would not have to wait long to have their day in a federal court. This development had much to do with the leadership of Senator Ellsworth. From its onset, the legislation creating the federal court system—remembered today as the Judiciary Act of 1789—has been attributed to Ellsworth's efforts. His colleagues in the First Congress attested to the Connecticut lawmaker's close connection to the bill. "My chum Ellsworth has been at it night and day these three months," wrote Georgia congressman Abraham Baldwin of the measure. Even opponents of the judiciary bill acknowledged Ellsworth's influence. "This Vile Bill is a child of his," opined Senator William Maclay of Pennsylvania.[5] James Madison also acknowledged Ellsworth's responsibility for the Judiciary Act of 1789. "The bill originated in the Senate," he recalled, "of which I was not a member, and the task of preparing it was understood, justly I believe, to have been performed by Mr. Ellsworth in consultation probably with some of his learned colleagues." "It may be taken for certain," Madison stated in a separate account, "that the bill organizing the judicial department originated in [Ellsworth's] draft, and that it was not materially changed in its passage into law."[6]

During the First Congress, Ellsworth worked with two Senate committees to construct the architecture and garner the necessary support for the judiciary bill. The first committee, which included one member from each of the ten states that had then sent a senator to New York, moved quickly to provide a general outline for a national court system. By the end of April 1789, less than a month after the full committee's creation, Ellsworth sent a report of the committee's progress to Richard Law, chief judge of Connecticut's Superior Court. According to Ellsworth's preliminary account, the senators agreed to create two types of federal courts—thirteen district courts and three circuit courts. The Senate adopted this general outline only weeks later. Although Ellsworth claimed no credit for the outline, at least one committee member, Senator Paine Wingate of New Hampshire, called Ellsworth the "leading projector" of the early plan.[7]

As soon as the full committee had agreed on the fundamentals, a second committee was tasked with turning the blueprint into a complete bill. This informal subcommittee included only three senators: William Paterson of New Jersey, Caleb Strong of

Massachusetts, and Oliver Ellsworth. The trio was likely selected because of their extensive legal experience. All were successful attorneys. Paterson had served for seven years as his state's attorney general. Strong was a well-heeled litigator with nearly twenty years experience at his state's bar.

It was also a congenial subcommittee. Ellsworth and Paterson had known each other since their undergraduate days at Princeton. The Princeton-educated attorneys reunited at the Constitutional Convention, where both supported the new plan of government but remained deferential to the states. As a constitutional delegate, the Irish-born Paterson had put forth the New Jersey Plan, which sought to amend, rather than replace, the Articles of Confederation. Under Paterson's proposal, each state would have continued to send an equally potent delegation to Congress, but the federal government would have been authorized to exercise various powers lacking under the Articles. Although he joined with the Connecticut delegation in voting against the New Jersey Plan, Ellsworth was an important advocate of the equal state vote in the Senate. With Senator Strong of Massachusetts Ellsworth shared fewer connections, but the two men were known to be friends, perhaps forging their relationship at the Constitutional Convention, where delegate Strong frequently joined Ellsworth in the camp of moderate nationalists.[8]

The trio worked well together. In mid-June, the subcommittee shared its draft measure with the full Senate. As first outlined and ultimately enacted, the judiciary bill consisted of three separate acts. One part addressed the role of the Supreme Court. A second part created circuit courts, while a third established federal district courts. Nonetheless, Senators Ellsworth, Paterson, and Strong imbued the bill with a single predominant purpose—to protect the nation's interests, which transcended the rights and privileges held by individual citizens. The landmark legislation was Ellsworth's best effort to create judicial harmony across the land.

The "Business of the Judicial Department"

The district courts were the first of the two new types of federal courts set forth in the three senators' draft bill. Under the trio's proposal, these courts were authorized to hear traditional admiralty disputes and suits brought to enforce federal tax and trade laws. In these cases there was broad political support for federal jurisdiction.

By 1789, the federal government already had nearly fifteen years of experience in settling admiralty disputes. Yet as Ellsworth had witnessed firsthand during his service in the Revolutionary-era Congress, the federal government lacked one critical tool this entire time: there were no federal *trial* courts for admiralty cases. The judiciary bill supplied this missing piece, authorizing the newly created federal district courts to exercise "exclusive original cognizance" over "all civil causes of admiralty and maritime jurisdiction."

Ellsworth and his fellow Senate drafters relied on the evidence that lawmakers could expand the federal government's power over admiralty cases without triggering partisan resistance. "The most bigoted idolizers of state authority have not thus far shown a disposition to deny the national judiciary the cognizance of maritime causes," the ardent nationalist Hamilton had been pleased to report during the ratification debates.[9] At Virginia's ratifying convention, Anti-Federalists George Mason and Patrick Henry had sharply criticized the proposed congressional power to create inferior courts. Even when Virginia ratified the Constitution in June 1788, its delegates simultaneously proposed to amend the Constitution in order to limit Congress's power to institute federal courts. But the Virginia ratifying delegates still made room for the creation of federal admiralty courts. Under their proposed amendment, "the Judicial Power of the United States" would be vested in the Supreme Court as well as "such Courts of Admiralty as the Congress may from time to time ordain." The ratifying delegates in New York and Pennsylvania passed similar amendments that would have limited Congress's power to create federal courts while expressly permitting it to institute admiralty courts. Recognizing such political consensus, the First Congress accepted without objection the proposal to close the long-standing gap in the federal government's ability to exercise its authority over admiralty cases.[10]

In the summary of the judiciary bill that he sent to Richard Law in April 1789, Ellsworth indicated that the proposed federal district courts would have admiralty jurisdiction. Six weeks later, when Ellsworth, Paterson, and Strong presented their draft bill to the Senate, a new clause extended the district court's jurisdiction to include "all seizures under laws of impost, navigation or trade of the United States." This additional jurisdictional grant, which was enacted as part of the final bill, gave the district courts the authority to enforce two related powers that now belonged to the federal government: the ability to tax Americans and regulate foreign trade.[11]

Whatever the nation's earliest leaders considered the proper level of taxation, there was general agreement on two issues: the government needed revenue, and federal courts were the proper means to enforce the nation's revenue system. "In a general view of the Matter," explained future customs collector Jeremiah Hill, "as there must be a Chain of Revenue Officers from one End of the United States to the other in order to secure the Government, protect the fair & honest Trader, and detect the Smuggler, so, it appears to me, there must be a line of Inferior Courts in the same Manner to protect those Officers, command Obedience to the federal Laws and ordinances & to punish Offenders." Massachusetts congressman Elbridge Gerry, who opposed the measure, nonetheless noted that the judiciary bill was "necessary to organize the government" so that "revenue could be provided for the support of public credit."[12]

The belief that federal courts were the appropriate enforcer of the nation's revenue laws was related to a notion shared by both supporters and opponents of a strong central government. According to Federal Farmer, an influential critic of the Constitution, the "business of the judicial department" was "faithfully to decide upon, and execute the laws, in judicial cases, between the public and individuals." Importantly, Federal Farmer concluded that to fulfill the responsibility of "executing the laws," courts needed to have the ability to decide cases in those areas where the legislature was authorized to make laws. Federal Farmer even applied this principle to the federal government, writing that it was "proper [that] the federal judiciary should have powers co-extensive with the federal legislature." Brutus, another leading Anti-Federalist, similarly acknowledged that the "judicial power should be commensurate with the legislative."[13] (Brutus is generally believed to have been Robert Yates of New York, but the identity of "Federal Farmer" remains a matter of contention. Once thought to be Richard Henry Lee of Virginia, Federal Farmer is today most often identified as Melancton Smith of New York.)

Federalist supporters of the Constitution agreed that the federal government's judicial power needed to be coextensive with its legislative powers. In one proratification essay, Ellsworth explained, "It is as necessary that there should be courts of law and executive officers, to carry into effect the laws of the nation, as that there be courts and officers to execute the laws made by your state assemblies." At the Constitutional Convention, James Madison likewise stated that "an effective Judiciary establishment commensurate to the legislative authority" was essential. John Dickinson of Delaware agreed. "If there was to be a National Legislature," remarked the London-schooled attorney, "there ought to be a national Judiciary."[14]

Although the taxing power was among the more controversial of the additional powers granted by the Constitution, Congress now clearly had the authority to raise revenue directly from Americans. The supporters of the judiciary bill thus characterized the creation of revenue courts as a step that Congress needed to take in order to use its new taxing power. While Senator Ellsworth was at work on the judiciary bill, Congressman James Madison accordingly predicted that the tax bill then under construction in the lower house would require "some special provision of a Judicial nature."[15]

As with the taxing power, there was broad political support behind empowering the federal government to regulate external trade. From Hamiltonian Federalists to Jeffersonian Republicans, the emerging consensus among the nation's post-Revolutionary leaders held that the present state of affairs called for a second declaration of independence, in which the American people would reorganize themselves under a stronger federal government that could protect their place among the European powers.

"You were told in the late war," Ellsworth wrote in one "Land-holder" essay, "that peace and Independence would reward your toil, and that riches would accompany the establishing of your liberties, by opening a wider market." Yet the lack of an effective power over foreign commerce had left Americans "dependent on every petty state in the world and on every custom house officer of foreign posts." A year before the Constitutional Convention, George Washington observed that popular antipathy toward British commercial restrictions would "facilitate the enlargement of Congressional powers in commercial matters, more than a half a century would otherwise have effected."[16]

Under Article I of the Constitution, Congress was enabled to enter into commercial treaties with foreign governments. The Articles of Confederation had also permitted Congress to negotiate foreign-trade agreements. The crucial difference was that the Constitution authorized Congress to enforce the commercial agreements that it made. Under the previous arrangement, the states had been responsible for enforcing the terms of the federal government's trade policy, including the embargoes that had been imposed on British goods throughout the struggle for independence.

Congress quickly moved to take advantage of its newly gained commercial powers. During the first session of Congress, James Madison introduced a bill to tax foreign imports. Madison's legislation showed that the new government's taxing and regulatory powers could be easily combined. His proposal was designed both to raise revenue for the new government and to retaliate against the largest source of American imports, Great Britain, for its restrictive trade policy toward the United States. Although Madison's proposal to use the tariff to discriminate against British trade failed in 1789, Thomas Jefferson's allies in Congress carried on the effort for the next decade. Indeed, the regulation of external commerce was an attractive foreign-policy tool for Jeffersonian Republicans, who sought to punish Great Britain for its mercantile policies without interfering with internal liberties. By shutting off its markets from the world, they contended that the American government could leverage the nation's power without having to challenge foreign sovereigns on the battlefield or even maintain a large military.

Potential benefits from the nation's commercial regulations still depended on their enforcement. As early as 1787, Ellsworth had concluded that empowering Congress to pass revenue and trade regulations required the creation of federal courts. "In all these matters and powers given to Congress," he wrote, "their ordinances must be the supreme law of the land, or they are nothing. They must have authority to enact any laws for executing their own powers, or these powers will be evaded by the artful and the unjust, and the dishonest trader will defraud the public."[17] Two years later, while the inaugural class of representatives debated the tariff bill, Ellsworth went to work formulating a national judiciary to enforce such commercial legislation. In the bill they delivered to the Senate, Ellsworth, Strong, and Paterson specified that the district courts would have the authority to hear seizure suits brought "under laws of impost, navigation or trade of the United States." As a result of the judiciary bill, the federal government had the means to prosecute those who breached the nation's trade laws— whatever they might be.

"The Very Vitals of It"

While lawmakers did not find fault with the jurisdiction granted to the district courts, proponents of the federal judiciary, including Ellsworth, would be compelled to compromise with critics over the remaining pieces of the nation's court system. Ellsworth and his draftsmen prompted an outcry when they recommended circuit courts to decide lawsuits between citizens who did not reside in the same state ("diversity" cases) and between foreign citizens and Americans ("alienage" cases). They were forced to tread carefully across a precarious political landscape. The provisions of the final bill concerning circuit courts speak again to Ellsworth's political aptitude.

Critics argued that the federal government had no business involving itself in alienage or diversity suits. Unlike the cases handled by the district courts, which might be brought to enforce a federal tax or trade law, the issue between the parties in a diversity or alienage suit could be as local as real estate. Opponents of an extensive federal court system might concede that cases involving certain federal laws were outside the province of the state courts, but they drew the line at disputes over commercial, property, and tort law. The state courts, they claimed, were competent to resolve common-law cases, even when the parties happened to be from different states or when one party happened to be a foreigner. "Justice may be obtained in [the state] courts on reasonable terms," insisted Federal Farmer. "I do not in any point of view see the need of opening a new jurisdiction to these causes."[18]

But many opponents of "party-based" jurisdiction had in mind a particular type of lawsuit. They wished to keep foreign—most often British—creditors from hauling American debtors to federal courts, which the Ellsworth committee's proposal would permit. At the political level, then, the circuit courts raised a topic of considerable debate throughout the American states: the proper treatment owed to British creditors.

Before the Revolutionary War, capital had been scarce in colonies such as Virginia. Under the typical arrangement, colonial planters borrowed the necessary capital from British creditors, promising them a share of the proceeds of their crop in return. This made indebtedness the ordinary state of affairs for planters throughout the southern colonies, as well as in the important northern colony of Massachusetts. Once the war began, the status of these debts was an issue that soon confronted state courts, lawmakers, and governors alike. Satisfying British creditors was not a high priority. In 1780, Maryland permitted its residents to discharge such debts by sending an equivalent sum in paper money to the state treasury. State courts throughout Revolutionary America proved hostile to the claims from abroad. From New Hampshire to North Carolina, several states shut the doors of their courts to British creditors.[19]

The 1783 Treaty of Paris, which ended the Revolutionary War, failed to resolve this dispute. Legislatures and courts of the several states simply refused to implement the treaty's provision holding that British creditors would not face impediments to the full recovery of the debts owed them. The prodebtor faction in Virginia's Assembly, for example, defeated an early effort to undo any state laws that contradicted the treaty's provisions. In Georgia and North Carolina, the courts refused to open their doors to creditor-suitors. When in the summer of 1786 a lawyer filed more than one hundred suits on behalf of a foreign client in a Maryland court, an angry mob persuaded the attorney to drop the suits and the judge to close the court.[20]

The Constitution offered a solution. Prior to ratification, the likelihood of a foreign creditor recovering his money varied from state to state. But under the Constitution's judiciary provisions, foreign debtors could avoid the state courts entirely. The federal judicial power had been extended to cases between parties of separate states and nations.

Not surprisingly, the political forces that had, up until the Constitution, succeeded in protecting American debtors, reacted negatively. The Constitution threatened to push American debtors into a new court system that would operate according to a different—and, many expected, procreditor—set of rules. Those sympathetic to America's debtors believed that the war with Great Britain had fundamentally altered the conditions of the credit relationships, and that therefore it was unfair to require Americans to honor their earlier obligations to British creditors. They wondered, in the words of George Mason, "If we are now to pay the debts due to British merchants, what have we been fighting for all this while?"[21]

Critics of diversity and alienage jurisdiction also pointed to the "cost" of establishing federal courts to hear these cases. And by cost, they referred to two separate realities. If Federalists wanted to facilitate the filing of diversity and alienage suits in federal courts, they would have to create and staff a large number of these venues, at a significant expense to federal taxpayers. To the individual litigant, on the other hand, it would be more costly if Congress created *fewer* federal courts, requiring a longer trip to the federal courthouse. There was, it seemed, no cheap way for Congress to recognize alienage or diversity jurisdiction.[22]

From Ellsworth's perspective, the controversy over whether to create federal courts to hear cases between Americans and foreigners was about the harmony that could come only if the federal government were made supreme over the "universal plan," the "grand and glorious scheme," "the whole intelligent system." These terms are those of Ellsworth's tutor Reverend Bellamy, not the senator. Bellamy used them to refer to God's governance over the world. But in an analogous sense, Ellsworth believed that in the grand matters of national interest there needed to be a competent authority, which could maintain peace between the separate parts of the union and carry the nation closer to the greatness for which it was destined.

From the time he was a delegate to the Continental Congress, the Connecticut lawmaker had contended that foreign policy was a federal issue with which the states were not to interfere. In January 1783, while serving in Congress, Ellsworth rejected an effort by delegate John Rutledge to lift the secrecy rule that governed the ongoing peace negotiations between American and British diplomats. The South Carolinian Rutledge was seeking to pass along to the residents of his state a letter written by Benjamin Franklin, one of the American ministers, concerning the obligations that Americans would owe to British creditors. Speaking against Rutledge's motion, which ultimately failed, Ellsworth warned that "a communication of this intelligence might encourage the States to extend confiscations to British debts, a circumstance which would be dishonorable to the United States and might embarrass a treaty of peace."[23]

Later in 1783, when the details of a preliminary peace treaty reached Philadelphia, Ellsworth teamed with congressional allies, including Alexander Hamilton of New York, to argue for the prompt recognition of the provisional agreement. Other congressional leaders argued that it was premature for the United States to ratify the preliminary treaty, which would not be final until Great Britain and France reached a separate peace agreement. In the face of this opposition, Ellsworth was, in the words of fellow delegate James Madison, "strenuous" for the "immediate execution of the Treaty."[24]

Throughout his final term in the Confederation Congress, Ellsworth continued to push for the federal government to take the lead in executing the provisional peace treaty. In early May 1783, General Washington had written Congress asking the delegates to deliver instructions "respecting the posts in the United States occupied by the British troops." Washington's recommendation was that "United States Troops" should move in as soon as the British evacuated, for fear that the forts "might be burned or destroyed by the Indians, or some other evil minded persons." Appointed to the committee responsible for replying to Washington's letter, Ellsworth submitted a proposal to Congress that tracked Washington's suggestion. Over objections by several Virginia delegates, who claimed that the Continental Army had no authority to occupy forts within their state, the delegates approved Ellsworth's plan.[25]

After Congress approved his proposal for federal occupation of the former British outposts, Ellsworth attempted to put a more controversial aspect of the preliminary treaty into operation. Under Article V of the provisional peace agreement, Congress was responsible for petitioning the states to return confiscated British property. According to Madison's records, on May 14, one month after Congress ratified the provisional treaty, Ellsworth and Alexander Hamilton "moved a call on the States, to fulfill the recommendation relative to the Tories." The joint effort was not the first time that the Connecticut and New York delegates had joined forces to call for federal enforcement of the provisional agreement. One month earlier, Ellsworth and Hamilton had demanded that Congress recommend the immediate release of British prisoners in compliance with another treaty provision.[26]

Before leaving Congress in the fall of 1783, Ellsworth remained confident that the United States would honor the terms of the peace treaty. On the day General Washington was scheduled to discuss the terms of the provisional agreement with General Guy Carleton, the commander of British forces in the United States, Ellsworth excitedly shared the news with Oliver Wolcott Sr., a former Connecticut governor and a relative of his wife. "Nothing as yet appears to induce a suspicion that the treaty will fail of being carried into execution on both sides as fast as the nature of the case will admit of," he wrote. "Certainly we cannot wish to see it violated and annulled." Ellsworth believed that the American peace negotiators had done quite well for the nation. "America, by the blessing of Heaven, which it becomes her most devoutly & greatly to acknowledge, has succeeded not less wonderfully in her negotiations than her arms," he reflected in the spring of 1783. "In short, she has imposed her own terms, & holds herself between Great Britain & France, as a Lady between two lovers, receiving from both favors which she could not have expected from either but from their mutual jealousy of being rivaled in her affections."[27]

The post-Revolutionary years dashed Oliver Ellsworth's hopes that the United States would honor its treaty commitments and receive favorable treatment from the major European powers. During his opening address at Connecticut's constitutional ratifying convention in 1788, Ellsworth cited the damage that the states had done to the nation's security by impeding British creditors from recovering their debts. Citing the foreign-policy imperatives that necessitated a stronger central government, he explained, "Another ill consequence of this want of energy is that treaties are not performed. The treaty of peace with Great Britain was a very favorable one for us. But it did not happen perfectly to please some of the states, and they would not comply with it. The consequence is, Britain charges us with the breach, and refuses to deliver up the forts on our northern quarter." If America did not pay back its debts, Ellsworth predicted, the nation's foreign creditors would "levy it by reprisals as the laws of nations authorize them."[28]

Ellsworth's objectives in arguing for alienage jurisdiction were to protect the individual rights of private creditors to recover on their contracts and the federal government's ability to enforce foreign treaties. South Carolina representative William Smith described a conversation that he had with Ellsworth when the First Congress was considering the judiciary bill. Asked by Smith to defend the sections of the bill that concerned alienage jurisdiction, Ellsworth replied that "the [constitutional] convention had in view the condition of foreigners when they framed the Judiciary of the United States. The Citizens were already protected by [the State] Judges and Courts, but foreigners were not. The Laws of the nations & Treaties were too much disregarded in the several states." Although Ellsworth began by referring to "the condition of foreigners," it was also the American people's national interest in maintaining good relations with foreign nations, he believed, that justified the extension of federal judicial review.[29]

In an oft-referenced floor speech at the Constitutional Convention two years earlier, Ellsworth had suggested that he did not consider the protection of the rights of individual citizens to be a relevant factor in the federal government's decision-making process. Ellsworth "turned his eyes for the preservation of his rights to the State governments." For the Connecticut Federalist, the federal government's responsibility for providing national security required it to place the common interest of the republic even before the economic welfare of individual citizens. While serving as chief justice of the United States, Ellsworth made this viewpoint explicit in *Hamilton v. Eaton* (1796), a well-known British creditor case. In *Hamilton*, the American debtor argued that, prior to the Treaty of

Paris, the lawmakers of North Carolina had forgiven his obligations to his British creditor. As a result, the American maintained that the federal treaty constituted an unjust interference with his property. The federal government was, in effect, asking him to pay a sum he no longer owed. Chief Justice Ellsworth conceded that the federal treaty demanded a sacrifice on the part of the debtor, but as his opinion candidly put it, "it is justifiable and frequent, in the adjustments of national differences, to concede for the safety of the state, the rights of individuals."[30]

From his entry into national politics, Ellsworth had maintained both that the general government needed protection and that individual rights could be regulated in the pursuit of civic harmony. These aspects of his political orientation disposed Ellsworth to support a compromise solution to the controversial matter of whether to grant every foreign creditor access to America's new federal courts. Guided by the Connecticut senator, the First Congress would reserve federal treatment only to those alienage and diversity cases of a certain magnitude.

The most important part of the compromise was adopted in the beginning stages of legislative parleying over the judiciary bill. In April 1789, the Grand Committee that formulated the general outline for the judiciary bill agreed to limit the diversity and alienage cases that could be brought in federal court to those where the "amount-in-controversy" was greater than five hundred dollars. Since 90 percent of the individual debts Americans owed to British creditors were for less than five hundred dollars, the amount-in-controversy minimum effectively closed the doors of the federal circuit courts to most of the politically charged alien-debtor cases.[31]

Nonetheless, when Senators Ellsworth, Paterson, and Strong submitted the draft judiciary bill, opponents tried to prohibit the federal government from entertaining *any* diversity or alienage cases. On June 22, 1789, Virginia's senators, Richard Henry Lee and William Grayson, offered an alternative plan that would confine the lower federal courts "to cases of admiralty and Maritime Jurisdiction." Compared with the subcommittee's bill, the key difference of the Virginia proposal was that it would strip diversity and alienage cases entirely from the jurisdiction of the lower federal courts. As a result, all foreign creditors would have to bring their suits in state courts, just as they had throughout the 1780s.[32]

Once the Virginians had presented their plan, Ellsworth rose immediately to defeat it. On the day that Lee and Grayson introduced their measure, Senator William Maclay recorded in his diary that "Ellsworth answered them and the ball was kept up until past three O'Clock." In replying to the Virginians, Ellsworth focused on Americans' common interest in preserving a central government and enforcing federal law. According to Senator Maclay's diary entry from the debate, "Elsworth [*sic*] on the Judiciary Says that there will be Attacks on the General Government that will go to the Very Vitals of it. Who then are to support the General Law?"[33] Along these same lines, South Carolina senator Pierce Butler recorded in his notes that Ellsworth believed that state judges would "swerve" in the face of political pressure against enforcing federal law. Prior to serving in the United States Senate, Ellsworth had been a state judge, so he knew whereof he spoke.[34]

The following day, Senator Paterson seconded Ellsworth's claim. In opposition to the Virginia proposal to use the state courts to try nearly all federal cases, Senator Paterson cited the rules under which state judges held their offices. In some states, judges were elected annually. This allowed the voters frequent opportunities to remove judges that enforced federal law. Thus, even if the state judges themselves did not "swerve," the power of the state electorates to retire state judges who enforced federal law might produce the same result: the "attacks" that Ellsworth feared on the "Very Vitals" of the federal government.

Unlike more ardent centralizers, Ellsworth and Paterson respected the position and competence of state officials. Paterson, of course, had shown his allegiance to the states by proposing his New Jersey Plan, which, if accepted, would have granted the states equal voting power in a unicameral Congress. The arguments of Ellsworth and Paterson were therefore persuasive. Two days after the Virginia proposal was raised, the Senate voted it down. Later in the summer, the five-hundred-dollar monetary requirement survived a similar effort in the House of Representatives to strip the federal courts from exercising any jurisdiction over alienage and diversity suits. In September, the amount-in-controversy requirement became a part of the first judiciary bill signed into law by President Washington.

The alienage and diversity provisions worked as Ellsworth and others had hoped they would. Suits brought by British creditors began filling the docket of the federal courts soon after the judiciary bill's enactment. In defense, American debtors continued to rely on state laws that purported to relieve them of their debts to British citizens. The federal courts, however, held the line and enforced the provisions of the peace treaty. In the five years that followed the Judiciary Act, British creditors prevailed in approximately five hundred cases before the Virginia circuit court. The federal courts, moreover, delivered the message that the federal government was supreme within the sphere of national policy. Reporting on one early creditor case brought in Ellsworth's home state, the *Connecticut Gazette* noted that the federal circuit court "adjudged that the statute law of Connecticut enabling the state courts to deduct [wartime] interest in [creditor] cases, was an infringement on the treaty of peace."[35] The compromise that provided some foreign creditors with access to federal courts also proved politically successful. Few losing parties in foreign creditor cases sought an appeal to the United States Supreme Court. Nor was there any sustained legislative effort in subsequent Congresses to strip the federal courts of jurisdiction over all alienage and diversity cases.[36]

"Cases of Great Magnitude"

A quarter century after the Judiciary Act became law, a famous Supreme Court opinion raised a separate issue as to the Judiciary Act's amount-in-controversy provision. According to the text of the Constitution, "the Judicial Power of the United States *shall extend* to cases between citizens of the United States and foreign nations." The question that the Supreme Court considered, but left unresolved, in the 1816 case of *Martin v. Hunter's Lessee* was whether this clause permitted *all* foreign creditors access to the federal courts, regardless of the size of their claim. (In *Martin*, the Court ruled that the Supreme Court's appellate power extended to cases heard on appeal from state courts. Justice Joseph Story's majority opinion also suggested that the framers intended for there to be some form of judicial review for *all* cases enumerated in the Constitution.)

Did the drafters of the judiciary bill calm a political storm only by circumventing a constitutional mandate? Ellsworth addressed the question in one 1787 proratification essay in which he wrote that nothing in the Constitution prevented Congress from authorizing that "all the cases, except the few in which [the Supreme Court] has original and not appellate jurisdiction, may in the first instance be had in the state courts and those trials be final except in cases of great magnitude."[37]

What the Connecticut attorney meant by "cases of great magnitude" is not clear. Most likely, Ellsworth believed that the framers had given the nation's lawmakers flexibility with regard to alienage cases and that the best course of action was to figure how far to extend the federal government's judicial power. Later, as a senator, he expressed no regret that the First Congress did not extend jurisdiction beyond the five-hundred-dollar limit. Consistent with his underlying conviction about the paramount need for the federal government to provide general security, he viewed the question of federal review principally in light of the federal government's need to withstand "attacks" against its "Very Vitals" and not in terms of the constitutional rights belonging to the litigants. The federal government could neither leave vital national interests entirely to the states nor overextend itself by providing a venue for every possible federal case. The federal government had to set priorities. Under the Judiciary Act of 1789, this is exactly what the First Congress did.

Still, some scholars contend that the authors of the Judiciary Act committed a constitutional foul when they failed to provide some form of federal review for all cases that could be heard in a federal court. Writing for the "mandatory view," legal scholar Robert N. Clinton argues that the framers intended "the congressional power under the so-called exceptions and regulations clause to consist of making both regulations for the implementation of the appellate jurisdiction vested in the Supreme Court by the Constitution and exceptions from that jurisdiction as seemed desirable *if and only if* [emphasis added] it had vested that portion of the judicial power of the United States either in original or appellate form in an inferior article III federal tribunal." Professor Clinton bolsters his argument with significant evidence of the framers' desire to assure "the supremacy of national law" and provide "a neutral forum" for the resolution of interstate and international concerns that affected "the peace and harmony of the national union." Unfortunately for the "mandatory view," Congress has continued the practice of keeping some "diverse" parties out of federal court. (Currently, the amount-in-controversy requirement for such cases is $75,000.) A lawsuit challenging the constitutionality of the requirement would settle the scholarly debate.

And it would not be the first time that a congressional provision dealing with the details of the judiciary fell to judicial scrutiny. In *Marbury v. Madison* (1803), which is famous for recognizing the federal judiciary's power to review the laws passed by Congress, the provision in question was from none other than the Judiciary Act of 1789. The *Marbury* Court held that Section 13 of the act unconstitutionally added to the Supreme Court's original jurisdiction, which the Constitution had limited only to "Cases affecting Ambassadors, other public Ministers and Counsels, and those in which a State shall be a Party." William Marbury, the plaintiff in the case, had brought instead a claim seeking a writ of mandamus, using Section 13 of the Judiciary Act (which authorized the Supreme Court to grant such writs) as his authority for proceeding directly to the high court.

Retired from federal office at the time of the decision, Ellsworth left no recorded comment as to his thoughts on Chief Justice John Marshall's majority opinion. One is left to wonder how *Marbury* would have been decided had Ellsworth, who resigned from the chief justiceship in 1800, been the Court's leader.[38]

"You Carry Law to Their Homes"

The amount-in-controversy compromise was not the only way in which proponents of federal judicial review reached out to those who objected, in particular, to the cost of trying all diversity and alienage cases before federal courts. Writing to Richard Law in April 1789, Ellsworth informed the Connecticut jurist of the structure proposed for the circuit courts. These courts, wrote Ellsworth, were "to consist of two Judges of the Supreme court & the district Judge."[39] The potential expense of the federal courts was a bone of contention for opponents of federal judicial power, but even supporters of a national court system did not want the judicial department to sap the treasury. Senator Caleb Strong, who later joined Ellsworth on the subcommittee that drafted the final bill, opined that the federal judiciary should be "as little expensive as possible."[40] By tasking district judges and Supreme Court justices to serve simultaneously as circuit court judges, the proposed and ultimately enacted configuration allowed for the creation of the circuit courts without hiring a single new federal judge.

The composition of the circuit courts also offered something to Federalists who aspired to extend the reach and enforcement of federal law. Under the judiciary bill, the nation was divided into three circuits, and sessions would annually be held in two separate locations within each circuit. Supreme Court justices were dispatched to these locations to hear the cases, a setup that gave the justices a broad geographical reach where their influence would be felt. "You carry Law to their Homes, to their very Doors," Senator Paterson boasted of the arrangement. By spreading out the locations to which Supreme Court justices traveled—by making the nation's judges, in Paterson's words, "meet every Citizen in his own State"—the crafters of the judiciary bill answered critics who claimed that a federal court system would force Americans to travel several hundred miles to the seat of their government to defend themselves in court. The particular judgments that the Supreme Court justices would deliver while riding circuit were also critical. Ellsworth explained that the circuit courts "would give system to the [judicial] department" and "uniformity to the proceedings." The rulings from these courts would permit Americans to order their affairs according to the legal interpretations provided by the justices of the Supreme Court. In this way, the organization of the circuit courts appealed to Federalists wishing to lengthen the arm of federal law.[41]

The types of cases that reached circuit court judges would be quite different from those brought before the district courts. The circuit courts were courts of general jurisdiction, whereas the district courts were limited to enforcing federal maritime and revenue regulations. Under the judiciary bill, the circuit courts were permitted to hear cases brought between Americans and foreign citizens, and between citizens of the separate states. The amount-in-controversy requirement was the only restriction on the subjects that could be decided in these cases, though of course this high-dollar limit meant that most tort claims would proceed in state courts. Senator Paterson predicted that the circuit courts would be likely to handle bigger-ticket disputes over "Money, Merchandize, Land bought and sold." The cases would be resolved by panels of three federal judges, with at least one vote from a Supreme Court justice necessary in every ruling.[42]

The circuit court's structure reflected a principle that Ellsworth had advocated in shaping the other branches of the federal government. At the Constitutional Convention, Ellsworth had supported frequent elections for senators, members of the House of Representatives, and the president. He championed more interaction between elected federal officials and their constituents. Ellsworth's home state was proof that an involved citizenry could cultivate through practice the habit of recognizing political talent, and that leaders who worked diligently for the trust of that citizenry could develop into capable statesmen, better attuned to the public good. While Ellsworth supported lifetime tenure for federal judges to ensure that the nation's constitutional commitments were maintained through periods of political fluctuation, he still supported a method of keeping these judges in frequent contact with the American people. The Judiciary Act provided that mechanism. By the end of President Washington's eight years in office, the justices of the Supreme Court had decided more than three thousand cases while riding circuit. As a result, the public had numerous opportunities to see Supreme Court justices in action, at trials held in federal circuit courts throughout the states.[43]

If the arrangement permitted the Supreme Court justices to extend their political clout, it also exposed them to political feedback. A decade after the Judiciary Act, Supreme Court justice Samuel Chase became the subject of public debate as he "roamed the Middle Circuit stamping out sedition wherever he could." In federal courthouses from New Jersey to Virginia, Justice Chase made clear that he would strictly enforce the controversial Sedition Act of 1798. Chase's conduct on the circuit made him a favorite target of the Republican press, which excoriated the justice as a "Lawyer . . . employed against the prisoner," "arbitrary, high handed and tyrannical," "an ungenerous and relentless judge," "a becoming spectacle . . . with a face like a full moon," and "naturally proud, imperious, & overbearing—positive in his dogmas—supercilious in his manners—prejudiced in his decisions—, and headstrong in his opinions." Outcry over Justice Chase's conduct while on circuit duty ultimately led to his impeachment by the United States House of Representatives, though he was acquitted by the Senate. At a time when it was not uncommon for federal courthouses to be "thronged with spectators from every quarter," the circuit courts brought Supreme Court justices to the American people, and vice versa.[44]

HIGH COURT CONSENSUS

Although the Senate's closed proceedings have prevented the compilation of a full historical record, there is evidence that Ellsworth was responsible for the final piece of the judiciary bill—that addressing the role of the early Supreme Court. When the Senate subcommittee of Ellsworth, Strong, and Paterson presented its complete bill, the measure bore the handwriting of each legislator. Notably, the portions of the Senate bill that pertained to the Supreme Court's jurisdiction were in Ellsworth's script. They also bear Ellsworth's signature in a more fundamental way. The sections defining the Supreme Court's "appellate jurisdiction"—the key aspect of the Supreme Court's authority—reflect the Connecticut senator's overall approach of limiting the powers of the federal government so that it could exercise them where it mattered most.[45]

The framers of the Constitution had already pointed Ellsworth to the crucial issue that he would have to determine. Unlike the federal district and circuit courts, the Supreme Court was not a congressional creation. It had been established by the Constitution, not the Congress. The framers had prescribed some of the

Supreme Court's duties. It was given "original jurisdiction" over certain legal disputes, thereby requiring the nation's justices to conduct trials in a small set of federal cases.

But the framers lobbed one major question over to Ellsworth and his peers in Congress. The Constitution also granted the Supreme Court appellate jurisdiction over the full range of cases within the federal government's jurisdiction, from the controversial alienage suits to cases that questioned the constitutionality of federal statutes. Since the Constitution had given the Supreme Court only a few types of cases that it was permitted to try and resolve in the first instance, the Court would be powerful primarily through the decisions it delivered on appeal. Yet under the Constitution, the Supreme Court could exercise appellate jurisdiction only after allowing for "such exceptions and under such regulations as the Congress shall make." Congress could thus decide to limit the Supreme Court's appellate jurisdiction by granting the lower federal courts the power to render final judgments in the federal cases assigned to them.

The manner in which Congress shaped the Supreme Court's appellate power had immediate political consequences. A broad grant of appellate authority would allow the justices of the Supreme Court to deliver verdicts in a variety of cases, setting a uniform rule that other courts would have to apply when facing the same issue. A narrower grant of appellate authority, on the other hand, would likely produce a greater amount of diversity in the applicable precedents in place throughout the nation. The Supreme Court's appellate powers raised the perennially controversial question of the proper relationship between the federal and state governments. By providing for a Supreme Court "with appellate jurisdiction," the Constitution created a tribunal that would have the power to decide cases brought to it from other courts. But the framers did not make explicit whether the state courts were within the Supreme Court's appellate jurisdiction, nor how the Supreme Court would go about hearing cases on appeal from them.

In 1789, an appeal from a lower court's decision meant something different from what it does today. In modern legal practice, an appeal begins once the trial of the lawsuit has ended. This was not the case at the end of the eighteenth century. As the late legal historian Wilfred J. Ritz noted, at the time the judiciary bill was debated, "an appeal was a part of the *trial* process. Just as the highest state courts were trial courts, so too an appeal to the highest state court was a procedure for obtaining either a trial in the first instance or a second or third trial in the state's highest court."[46]

What made appeals controversial to late eighteenth-century Americans was that by allowing for *new* trials, they shifted power away from the citizen-jurors who first tried the case to appellate judges—politically appointed government officials who were empowered to disregard all prior verdicts. For this reason, critics of the Constitution's judicial provisions took aim at the Supreme Court's appellate authority. They pointed out that the Constitution extended the appellate jurisdiction of the Supreme Court to questions of "law and fact." The power to reestablish the facts of a case authorized the Supreme Court to hear evidence and examine witnesses. The evidence and the witnesses could have been presented earlier at trial or for the first time before the justices of the Supreme Court. Either way, to critics, the right to re-present one's case before the nation's highest court rendered meaningless the previous decisions reached by the civilian jury. "The appeal to the [Supreme Court]," complained Maryland Anti-Federalist Luther Martin, "is *to decide not only* on the law but on the fact. . . . If, therefore, *even* in *criminal* cases the general government is not satisfied with the verdict of the jury, its officer may remove the prosecution to the supreme court, and *there* the *verdict of the jury is to be of no effect.*" Although he supported the Constitution, Edmund Pendleton complained on the floor of Virginia's ratification convention about the extension of appellate authority to "both law and fact," preferring that the provision "had been buried in oblivion." James Madison, meanwhile, reminded skeptical delegates that Congress could foreclose the threat of "vexatious appeals."[47]

Martin and others predicted that through the Supreme Court's appellate jurisdiction, civilian juries would be replaced by juryless procedures. Acting alone, the justices of the Supreme Court would decide the cases that they reheard on appeal. This assessment was based both on the text of the Constitution and recent experience. The Constitution did not require a jury to be present in any of the cases brought to the Supreme Court on appeal. There was also relevant precedent. As early as 1780, Congress had shown its willingness to create juryless federal appellate courts, at the suggestion of Oliver Ellsworth.

As a member of the Continental Congress during the Revolutionary War, Ellsworth had been one of the delegates assigned to creating the first federal courts of appeals. These courts were created in the wake of the *Active* case, as discussed in Chapter 2. This lawsuit motivated the Revolutionary-era Congress to create a federal court to hear admiralty suits on appeal from the states. Prior to the creation of these appellate courts, Congress itself had been responsible for reviewing admiralty appeals. In another difference from today, it was not rare at the end of the eighteenth century for appeals to proceed before legislatures or executive officials. In Ellsworth's Connecticut, as in other American states, a party could appeal certain cases to the General Assembly.

The controversy over the *Active* case convinced Congress to delegate the function of reviewing admiralty cases to an appellate court. In January 1780, Ellsworth presented the plan for how the court of appeals in cases of capture would operate. An appeal before this appellate tribunal would entail another trial. Ellsworth's plan provided "that a court be established for the trial of all appeals" from the state admiralty courts. Moreover, the "trials therein" would "be according to the usage of nations and not by jury." The congressional delegates overwhelmingly moved by a vote of ten to two to approve the plan, setting a precedent that federal appellate courts need not include civilian juries.[48]

Those who feared the Constitution's judicial provisions were concerned with protecting the political power of the citizen-jurors as well as the rights of the individual litigants. Among eighteenth-century Americans, there was considerable support for granting entities outside of the federal government a role in the nation's public life. States' rights may be the most recognized example of a division of power between federal and nonfederal bodies, but they are not the only one. Civilian juries, like the states, exercised considerable sovereignty within their own political terrain. In the words of Anti-Federalist writer Federal Farmer, civilian juries "secure[d] to *the people at large*, their just and rightful controul in the judicial department." At the time, jurors had a right to participate "both in making and executing the laws." In so doing, they gave the public its rightful role in the administration of justice.[49]

Naturally, proponents of the "transcendent privilege" entailed in a jury trial believed that once the civilian jurors reached a verdict, the outcome should hold. To allow appellate judges to retry cases was to reallocate political power from civilian jurors to federally appointed judges, from those who would experience the application of the law as citizens to those who served as officers of the government. The debate over the proper extent of the Supreme Court's appellate jurisdiction ran through the ratification of the Constitution and continued in the spring of 1789, when Ellsworth went to work crafting the Judiciary Act. Although the Supreme Court existed only on paper, the potential that it would efface that "palladium of liberty"—the civilian jury—had already made the Supreme Court a controversial subject.

As with other matters, the Grand Committee laid the framework for a compromise. Writing at the end of April, Ellsworth mentioned a pair of provisions contained in the general outline adopted by the senators. Six weeks later, both were present in the complete bill presented to the full Senate. The first item, written in Ellsworth's hand, required a "petition in error" to gain Supreme Court review of a civil action that had been earlier tried at the circuit level. Requiring parties to seek a "petition in error" (or a "writ of error" in the final bill) would limit the Supreme Court to considering only legal questions. Justices were prohibited from reexamining the facts of the case found at trial. In addition, the final bill made eligible for review only cases where the amount-in-controversy exceeded two thousand dollars.[50]

This provision responded to another objection of those who believed that the Constitution insufficiently limited the Supreme Court's appellate jurisdiction. Because appeals before the Supreme Court would be heard at the nation's capital, "parties must travel many hundred miles," charged the Anti-Federalist pamphleteer Brutus, "with their witnesses and lawyers, to prosecute or defend a suit; no man of middling fortune, can sustain the expense of such law suit, and therefore the poorer and middling class of citizens will be under the necessity of submitting to the demands of the rich and the lordly." The two-thousand-dollar amount-in-controversy floor eliminated the possibility that small suits between citizens of different states, or between Americans and their foreign creditors, could be appealed to the Supreme Court. In such cases, the parties would have to accept a lower court's judgment. There would be no "intolerable" appeals to the Supreme Court of ordinary matters between private litigants, as Brutus had feared.[51]

The scope of the Supreme Court's authority to reverse the judgments of the state courts posed a final challenge to the drafters of the Judiciary Act. The general outline that the senators had adopted in April 1789 had provided for federal courts authorized to handle particular areas of federal law. But other areas of federal law—most notably, suits asserting rights under the Constitution or federal statutory law—fell outside these categories and therefore could not be enforced through the federal district or circuit courts. Ellsworth addressed this matter in Section 25 of the judiciary bill, which pertained to the Supreme Court's appellate jurisdiction over the state courts. Section 25 declared that the state courts would have the authority to entertain all federal cases that had not been assigned to a federal court. The same section also empowered the Supreme Court to review the state court rulings in these cases.

Section 25 conferred on the state judiciaries the responsibility to enforce certain areas of federal law. Among the federal cases that would be tried in state courts were those that turned on one party's claim to relief under the Constitution itself. The Judiciary Act, however, did not create a lower federal court where a party could challenge a state that had impaired a private contract. Section 25 made clear that the state courts would be responsible for the enforcement of constitutional provisions, including those that protected citizens from the actions of the state governments, such as the prohibition against laws impairing contractual obligations. Also among the federal cases that Section 25 directed to the state trial courts were those based on "the laws of the United States." This meant that when Congress enacted a statute, the state courts would ordinarily be responsible for enforcing the federal law. Reflecting another of Ellsworth's principles, Section 25 directed the Supreme Court to review the state courts only when they refused to recognize the federal claim. Where a state court opted to enforce the federal statute or constitutional provision at issue in the case, a party who disagreed with the court's application of the federal law would have no right to appeal to the Supreme Court.

By allowing the state judiciaries to try cases based on federal law, Ellsworth moderated the federal government's enforcement power. He did so by adopting a generally Anti-Federalist posture rather than one that would have increased the role of the potentially controversial lower federal courts. Voicing this latter position, Edmund Randolph, who served as the nation's first attorney general under President Washington, believed that the drafters of the judiciary bill should have accepted the Constitution's invitation and directed all cases that arose under a federal statute to proceed directly to a federal court.[52] Anti-Federalists strongly disagreed. They believed that where Congress had the right to act, it could create courts to enforce the laws that it passed. "The cases affecting ambassadors, public ministers, and consuls—of admiralty and maritime jurisdiction; controversies to which the United States are a party, and controversies between states," acknowledged Brutus, "should be under the cognizance of the courts of the union, because none but the general government, can, or ought to pass laws on their subjects." Yet Brutus and other Anti-Federalists also claimed that the state courts were up to the task of enforcing the laws that Congress passed. "So far as I have been informed," remarked Brutus, "the courts of justice in all the states, have ever been found ready, to administer justice with promptitude and impartiality according to the laws of the land." They had faith in state judges. Even James Madison predicted at the Virginia ratification convention that ordinarily "the far greater number of cases—ninety-nine out of a hundred, will remain with the State Judiciaries."[53]

If anyone could not be trusted to enforce "the laws of the land" fairly, it was federal judges. Anti-Federalists predicted that federal judges could be relied upon to uphold federal statutes even when they exceeded constitutional powers. They would interpret the Constitution, remarked Brutus, "not only according to its letter, but according to its spirit and intention; and having this power, they would strongly incline to give it such a construction as to extend the powers of the general government, as much as possible, to the diminution, and finally to the destruction of that of the respective states." Federal judges would thus hasten the erosion of the original plan for a federal government of enumerated powers.[54]

According to Brutus, a solution to the eventuality (in his eyes) of federal judicial passivity in face of national power was to permit the state courts to hear all cases where the claims of the parties were based on a federal statute or constitutional provision. "I see every case that can arise under the constitution or laws of the United States, ought in the first instance to be tried in the court of the state," he wrote. To this recommendation, however, Brutus added an important proviso. "The state courts would be under sufficient controul," he noted, "if writs of errors were allowed from the state courts" responsible for hearing the cases in the first instance "to the supreme court of the union." Such an arrangement, Brutus concluded, "would preserve the good old way of administering justice, would bring justice to every man's door, and preserve the inestimable right of trial by jury."[55]

In Section 25, Ellsworth pursued the course of action that Brutus had recommended. The Connecticut Federalist accepted the Anti-Federalist's suggestion that allowing the state courts to try cases based on federal statutory or constitutional claims, subject to oversight by the Supreme Court, struck the right balance. Under Section 25, if the state court ruled that the federal government had exceeded its constitutional powers, the losing party would have to appeal the case to the Supreme Court. The burden of traveling to the seat of the national government to obtain review limited the appeals to cases where the litigant was sufficiently interested and confident that the federal right would be upheld. In this way, distance acted as a deterrent to federal overreach, much as the amount-in-controversy requirement had done. In both cases, the restrictions reserved the use of federal judicial power for the most important cases.

Ellsworth's crafting of Section 25 disarmed the potential opposition to the Supreme Court's appellate jurisdiction. It encountered no objection in either the Senate or the House. Enacted into law, Section 25 provided the early Supreme Court few opportunities to review cases on appeal from the state courts. It took five years before a single case reached the Supreme Court under this provision, and in its first decade of existence the Court handled only seven such cases.[56] The short supply of appeals from the state courts was a triumph for Ellsworth's legislative strategy. He had hoped that the Supreme Court would have few opportunities to show its strength to the state courts. As he wrote to Richard Law during the summer of 1789, "frequent reversals" by the Supreme Court "would probably more hurt" the "feelings" and "influence" of the state courts. By limiting the potential points of friction between federal and state courts, Ellsworth once again hoped to achieve the kind of harmony—here between the two levels of American government—that showed that the hand of providence was guiding the body politic.[57]

"A Perfect Uniformity"

In July 1789, one month after the drafting committee of Ellsworth, Strong, and Paterson had presented its handiwork, the Senate voted fourteen to six to approve the judiciary bill. The crucial elements of the subcommittee's draft survived. The federal court system would be a three-tiered structure, with the district courts trying admiralty and revenue cases, the circuit courts hearing important civil suits and federal crime cases, and the Supreme Court exercising review power over the legal judgments in specified cases for which appeals were granted. During the same session, the House approved the Senate's judiciary bill with minimal alterations by a margin of thirty-seven to sixteen.[58]

In August 1789, Ellsworth wrote to Richard Law that "dividing the ground" between the federal and state courts had proven difficult, but he was confident that no plan "more economical, systematic, and efficient" could be found. In this letter, the Connecticut senator summarized the challenge that he had faced. It was clear to the leaders of the early Congress that the judicial power of the nation needed to be divided so that the federal government could decide certain cases. But it was also clear that the allocation of power to the federal government had to be done with minimal expense and without interfering with the proper domain of the states.[59]

During the debate over whether to ratify the Constitution, Ellsworth had written that federal courts were needed to enforce the nation's laws consistently: "A perfect uniformity must be observed thro' the whole union . . . [and] for a uniformity one judiciary must pervade the whole." The uniformity that he provided in the Judiciary Act was limited. The federal government now had venues to enforce essential federal laws, including the national impost, and to resolve certain disputes that, if resolved elsewhere, threatened national peace and security, such as the sizable British creditor cases. For Ellsworth, harmony was not achieved through uniform nationalization, but the prudent division of decision-making authority between the federal and state governments. Thus would prosper the "whole intelligent (American) system."[60]

CHAPTER SIX

CASES AND CONTROVERSIES

Look not to the opinions of men, but their actions; and weigh them,
not in the scales of passion, or of party, but in a legal balance.

—Chief Justice Oliver Ellsworth, Charge to the Grand Jury of the
Circuit Court for the District of South Carolina, May 7, 1799

IN MARCH 1794, SENATOR ELLSWORTH MET PRIVATELY WITH PRESIdent Washington to brief the chief executive on an urgent proposal that Ellsworth had crafted with a cadre of Senate allies who called themselves the "Friends of Peace." Over the course of the five years since the inaugural class of lawmakers had been seated, early legislation, including Ellsworth's Judiciary Act, had invigorated the framers' plan of government. Yet much remained the same—in particular, the concern that the Revolution had not completely secured American independence.

The era in which the United States would stretch from sea to shining sea remained in the distant horizon. France, Spain, and various Native American tribes still laid claim to much of what is now the United States, while England maintained one thousand redcoats on American soil. The presence of foreign nations on the North American continent and the enduring concern with the strength of the U.S. government gave rise to a pair of related questions that shaped national politics in the decade following ratification: how was national independence and how was domestic harmony to be preserved?

Throughout the 1790s, Ellsworth would respond to these questions as a senator, the nation's chief justice, and finally as a diplomat dispatched by President John Adams on a controversial mission to Napoleon-led France. And for Ellsworth, their answer lay outside the tenets favored by either of the decade's dominant political camps. As before, political prudence was the Connecticut Federalist's solution.

PLANNING THE JAY TREATY

The Jay Treaty of 1794 provides the context for Ellsworth's most important accomplishment as a senator during the early 1790s. Prior to the Louisiana Purchase, this settlement with Britain was the nation's most consequential and controversial international accord. The Jay Treaty prevented a second Anglo-American war from erupting, but critics charged that it subverted American independence. Ellsworth's efforts in securing the Jay Treaty displayed a key element of his political framework—namely, that peace should not be risked for idealism alone.

The genesis of the Jay Treaty can be traced to 1792 when war between Britain and France reignited. Among its wartime measures, the British government authorized the capture of American ships carrying agricultural staples to French-held ports. When Congress convened in January 1794, Representative James Madison presented his colleagues with a plan for retaliation—a steep tariff on British imports to the United States. For Madison, the discriminatory duties against Great Britain advanced a larger political cause. Free commerce was an essential principle of the American Revolution.

Several years earlier, in *Federalist* 10, Madison had explained how a large federal republic diluted the political power of otherwise potent narrow interests, who might dominate a smaller territory. The Virginia congressman here applied the same concept in another context. The tariffs on British commerce would produce not a larger republic but a larger marketplace. The increased competition for American trade resulting from the duties on British imports would open up new avenues for international trade, while pressuring Great Britain to loosen its restrictions on American commerce. In the same way that larger political republics produced an enlightened equilibrium with respect to domestic policies, an enlarged commercial marketplace would reduce the artificial trade barriers set by self-interested foreign governments, leading to the same enlightened equilibrium with respect to the prices exchanged for economic goods.

The retaliatory tariff against Great Britain reflected the strong current of foreign-policy idealism in the Democratic-Republican Party, which was coalescing around a shared belief that America should remain true to its Revolutionary ideals even if it meant alienating its largest trading partner. Democratic-Republican foreign policy leaned in the direction of taking unilateral action against Britain, cutting off trade with a nation that violated the republican principle of free commerce in the fruits of one's labors. The anti-British sentiments of the early idealists ran deep. Many of them were southerners still affected by the brutal fighting that gripped their region in the final chapter of the Revolutionary War. The attempts by British creditors to recoup their debts in the immediate aftermath of the war further embittered their southern trading partners. In the early 1790s, the Democratic-Republicans coupled their bias against Great Britain with a fondness for France, whose republican revolutionaries had brought a bloody end to the country's ruling monarchy. At home and abroad, America's early Democratic-Republican idealists sought freedom, an end state in which the federal government intervened minimally in the domestic economy while taking a stand against foreign powers that opposed free international commerce.

Pitted against the Democratic-Republicans was the Federalist Party, a political camp whose ranks included Oliver Ellsworth. Federalists adopted what they considered a practical approach to foreign policy. The most committed proponent of Federalist realpolitik was Madison's *Federalist* coauthor Alexander Hamilton. In the early republic, Hamilton spearheaded a fiscal program aimed at increasing American wealth while protecting the fledgling nation against foreign nations opposed to U.S. interests. The Federalists favored a more cautious policy toward Great Britain, America's principal trading partner, since they relied on a steady stream of foreign imports to maintain the nation's public finances. Without the revenue generated from British imports, the United States would have to find some other way to keep up with the interest payments that the nation owed on its Revolutionary-era debts. In 1790, furthermore, Congress voted to add the states' outstanding debts to the federal government's balance sheet. By adding to the national government's debt, the Hamiltonian plan also increased the need for a reliable tax revenue source.

The "Friends of Peace" Triumph

Two months after Madison proposed discriminatory duties against Great Britain, the Federalists had all but defeated this hard-line approach. The initial popular uproar over Britain's restrictive policy had subsided. Yet news of a new British order shifted the political scales once again, generating renewed cries for retaliation. Under this order, which reached Congress in March 1794, Britain declared that its warships would seize American vessels attempting to carry any cargo to the French West Indies. Congressional Federalists feared war with Great Britain. At this critical moment, four northeastern senators, including Ellsworth, entered the fray. Their decisive action would contribute to a crucial chapter in the nation's early diplomatic history.

Days after reports of the new British order reached Philadelphia, Ellsworth gathered with Senators George Cabot and Caleb Strong of Massachusetts in the residence of Senator Rufus King of New York. According to King's notes, the Federalist senators came together out of a shared fear "that war might and probably would be the consequence of these aggressions of England, unless some system calculated to calm the public mind, as well as the public councils, was speedily adopted." The anti-British uproar, the Senate quartet was convinced, had sprung not from the reasonable judgments of the American public but from a "Fraction opposed to the Government," which was using the news of the British policy to "embarrass and derange" the Washington administration. In the face of this partisan demand for war, this Federalist foursome felt it was their duty to determine a more prudent course. King referred to his fellow conferees accordingly as the "Friends of Peace."[1]

Without delay, the four Federalists began sketching what would become the Washington administration's plan for averting war. They proposed that the president dispatch an "Envoy extraordinary" to London. For the emergency diplomatic mission to succeed, the Friends of Peace understood, it was necessary to pick the right minister. "Unless a person possessing Talents of the first order, enjoying the confidence of the Friends of Peace and of the Government, and whose character was unexceptional in England was selected," they reasoned, "it would be fruitless to make an appointment." The Friends of Peace settled on Treasury Secretary Alexander Hamilton. Ellsworth brought the plan to President Washington.[2]

For Ellsworth, the political calculus was simple. He maintained that the refusal by southern partisans to permit British creditors to collect debts was behind the animosity between Great Britain and the United States. By agreeing to allow the British to collect the sums due them, the United States could preserve the fruits of independence. "The debts of the South, which were, doubtless among the causes of the late revolution, have ever since operated to obstruct its benefits," Ellsworth wrote to Oliver Wolcott Jr. in April 1794. "Under these auspices, an extensive combination of the wicked and weak has been arranged for some time past, and will probably continue its efforts to disturb the peace of this country." A special envoy who could reassure British creditors of their rightful claims against American debtors, Ellsworth concluded, could "save us from war."[3]

Believing that war with Britain was best avoided, President Washington endorsed the plan outlined by the Friends of Peace. At the same time, however, Washington doubted that Hamilton was the right envoy. In Washington's assessment, Hamilton "did not possess the general confidence of the Country" on account of his centralizing fiscal policies, which were unpopular in Democratic-Republican strongholds. Nevertheless, Washington kept his treasury secretary under consideration. The following month, Washington told Senator Robert Morris of Pennsylvania that he was still deciding among Hamilton, Vice President John Adams, recently retired Secretary of State Thomas Jefferson, and Chief Justice John Jay, who was a seasoned diplomat from his Revolutionary assignments in Madrid and London. Hearing Washington's list, Morris advised eliminating Adams and Jefferson. A week later, the decision was all but made for Washington when Hamilton sent the president a letter concluding that Jay was the best choice. As it happened, Jay was in the nation's capital when Hamilton's letter reached the president, allowing Washington to offer the chief justice the assignment in person.

The following day, the Friends of Peace made their own visit to Jay, hoping to convince the New York lawyer to accept the post with haste, believing that "the situation of the Country [was] too interesting and critical to permit him to hesitate."[4] They also counseled Jay on negotiating with Great Britain. Specifically, the senators advised Jay to steer clear of pressuring Britain to lift its trade restrictions, suggesting a more modest approach—an agreement that reiterated the terms of the peace treaty that had ended the Revolutionary War. The Federalist cadre informed Jay that it would be unnecessary and unwise to seek official guidance from the full Senate. Favoring a larger role for the executive branch, which would ultimately draft Jay's formal instructions, and a smaller role for their own body, the Friends of Peace requested that the resulting treaty be "signed subject to the appropriation of the Senate," as required by the Constitution.[5]

This advice to Jay was a mixture of principle and politics. Federalist politicians generally supported the notion that in the realm of diplomacy the executive could exercise a certain degree of power without approval from the other branches. As a practical matter, the Friends of Peace feared that their colleagues might nullify the intended effect of the mission—the securing of peace—

by saddling the envoy with unrealistic demands. Ellsworth was confident that by avoiding a heated congressional debate over the appropriate boundaries for the negotiation, his allies had secured a critical victory. In a letter to Oliver Wolcott Jr. in June 1794, the Connecticut senator reflected,

> I suggested to you the idea of turning our grievances into a channel of negotiation. I now venture to assure you that Mr. Jay will be sent as a special Envoy to the Court of London, with such powers and instructions as probably will produce the desired effect. . . . This, Sir, will be a mortifying movement to those who have endeavored, by every possible means, to prevent a reconciliation between this country and Great Britain.[6]

The successful departure of the Jay mission was due primarily to the efforts of Ellsworth and his close Senate allies. According to diplomatic historian Joseph Ralston Hayden,

> Probably the outstanding point in connection with the negotiation of the treaty . . . is the extent to which a small group of Federalist Senators, who were also among Washington's most trusted advisers, dominated the entire proceeding. These men suggested the mission; they secured its acceptance by the President, and practically directed the selection of the envoy; they secured his confirmation by the Senate; they sent him out fully cognizant of their views as to what sort of treaty should be striven for and under very flexible instructions from the Department of State.

When the veteran diplomat Jay set sail once again for London, the Friends of Peace had reason to celebrate—for the moment, at least.[7]

DEBATE OVER THE TREATY

In March 1795, one year after the plan for a peace envoy was hatched in Senator King's room, John Jay returned to present President Washington the results of the treaty talks. Washington agreed to keep the terms of the agreement secret until ratification. Following its closed debate, the Senate approved the Jay Treaty in another party-line vote of twenty to ten, with all Federalists supporting and all Democratic-Republicans voting to reject the measure. The ratified treaty, now the "supreme law of the land" pursuant to the Constitution's grant of elevated status to such agreements, was then released to the American public, which had been kept in the dark about the terms of Jay's mission.

The Friends of Peace must have been astonished by the widespread outrage at the Washington administration for having agreed to the terms with Great Britain that these Federalist insiders had suggested. As instructed first by the Friends of Peace, and later by the administration, Jay followed a conciliatory path with his British counterparts. Rather than imposing the retaliatory tariffs that Madison proposed, the Jay Treaty pledged that the United States would impose no higher duties on British imports than it levied on goods from other nations. The treaty lifted British restrictions on American commerce to the West Indies only temporarily, limiting the period of free trade there to two years. In return, Jay secured two principal benefits. First, Britain pledged to evacuate its northwest posts. Second, the very act of reaching an agreement had averted the immediate possibility of war. When the terms of the treaty were publicized, however, crowds from Boston to Charleston gathered to protest the agreement as outrageously pro-British. It was remarked that Jay could traverse the American landscape day or night without a lamp: ample illumination would be provided by all the effigies burning in protest of his treaty.

Prior to the treaty's publication, it was not only the American public that had been kept from appraising the terms of Jay's agreement. The Washington administration and the Federalist-led Senate had afforded no role to the public's representatives in the lower house of Congress. During the summer of 1795, Democratic-Republican leaders in the House of Representatives, including Madison, considered ways to assert their will. The president, meanwhile, bided his time. When the House returned to the Capitol in December, Washington informed Congress that British approval of the treaty had not yet arrived. By early 1796, Democratic-Republican purists were willing to wait no longer. "Persuaded of the fatal effects of delay," Representative Edward Livingston of New York demanded that Washington disclose the instructions that his administration had given Jay.[8]

The deliberation over the Livingston motion revealed the active role that Ellsworth played in both chambers of Congress. Although the measure was raised in the House, the Connecticut senator was present at a caucus of Federalist congressmen during the initial considerations of Livingston's motion. According to Representative Theodore Sedgwick, a Massachusetts Federalist, Ellsworth had advised his House allies to oppose the Livingston measure. Convinced that a majority of members already supported the resolution, the Federalist leaders opted against organizing a resistance to Livingston's demand. For Ellsworth, the unsuccessful meeting was the last time he would be able to assert his legislative sway as the de facto leader of the Federalist majority in the Senate.[9]

CHIEF JUSTICE ELLSWORTH

After returning from London, John Jay retired from the Supreme Court to become governor of New York. President Washington nominated the seasoned politician John Rutledge to succeed Jay as chief justice. But support for the former Constitutional Convention delegate evaporated when reports reached the Federalist Senate that Rutledge, then serving as the chief justice of South Carolina, had recently given an incendiary speech against the Jay Treaty. Following the Senate's rejection of Rutledge, Washington turned to Patrick Henry, but his fellow Virginian declined the nomination. William Cushing, a sitting Supreme Court justice, also refused the chief justice position.

Finally the president opted for Senator Ellsworth. On March 8, 1796, the day after receiving the nomination, the Senate confirmed Ellsworth as chief justice of the Supreme Court by a vote of twenty-one to one, with only Virginia's Stevens T. Mason, the nephew of the late Anti-Federalist statesman George Mason, voting against the nominee. "No appointment in the U.S.," commented Congressman Jeremiah Smith, a New Hampshire Federalist, "has been more wise or judicious. [Ellsworth] is a very able lawyer, a very learned man, a very great Politician, & a very honest man. In short, he is every thing one would desire."[10]

Ellsworth was ambivalent about becoming chief justice since it meant retiring from the Senate. Ellsworth took the trouble of explaining his decision in a letter to Connecticut's Governor Oliver Wolcott Sr. "It is, Sir, my duty to acquaint you that I have, with some hesitation, accepted an appointment in the Judiciary of the United States, which of course vacates my seat in the Senate. This step, I hope, will not be regarded as disrespectful to a State which

I have so long had the honour to serve and whose interests must forever remain precious to my heart." Given his strong attachment to his home state, nothing indicates that Ellsworth's reservations over leaving his post as one of Connecticut's two selected representatives in the Senate were less than heartfelt.[11] John Adams, who as Washington's vice president presided over the Senate, later regretted the void that Ellsworth left there. In Adams's estimation, Democratic-Republican activists waged a steady campaign "to explode Washington, to sacrifice Adams, and bring in Jefferson. . . . Washington was aware of this, and prudently retreated. But what had he done before he left the chair? Ellsworth, the firmest pillar of his whole Administration in the Senate, he had promoted to the high office of Chief Justice of the United States." Had Ellsworth, King, and Strong—all senators during Washington's tenure—been in the same position during Adams's administration, "the world would never have heard of the disgraceful cabals and unconstitutional proceedings of that body," Adams concluded, referring to Democratic-Republican mischief.[12]

Despite his retirement from the Senate, Ellsworth still assisted the Washington administration from his new perch atop the federal judiciary. Ellsworth's rapid confirmation as chief justice came a week after Representative Livingston had moved to make public the administration's diplomatic papers. In later eras, Ellsworth's position as chief justice would have barred him from weighing in on the Jay Treaty. But the wall of formal separation between officials in the three federal branches had not been constructed in the 1790s. When Ellsworth became chief justice, the United States government was still in its start-up phase. With no class of professional functionaries to fill the various federal posts, national leaders moved easily from one federal branch to another. To be sure,

Federalists and Democratic-Republicans sought an independent federal judiciary. Agreeing that "no one was the best judge of his own cause," both camps settled on the rule that different persons should not simultaneously serve on the federal bench and in the political branches, temporary exceptions aside. But what mattered more than the rule was the reason behind it: that the federal courts must apply federal law impartially. This allowed some leeway for federal judges to express their views on congressional enactments, even if such perspectives were offered outside a formal judicial proceeding.

Political realities aside, Ellsworth was among the most practical members of the founding generation. The veteran Federalist would not let the opportunity pass to dash off a cogent memorandum on the Livingston proposal to former Senate colleagues, and ultimately the president himself.

Five days after becoming chief justice, Ellsworth drafted a response to the Livingston motion. Although addressed to Connecticut senator Jonathan Trumbull Jr., the nine-page document did not read as a personal missive between familiar parties. Dispensing with any greeting to the addressee, Ellsworth began instead by citing a constitutional provision. By demanding Jay's instructions, a clear majority in the House of Representatives had asserted its will. Yet Ellsworth argued that the House did not have the constitutional authority to demand treaty instructions from the executive branch. After all, the framers had granted the treaty-making power exclusively to the president and the United States Senate, leaving the House no right to monitor the process or gain access to the envoy's instructions.

Two weeks after Ellsworth dispatched his memorandum to Senator Trumbull, President Washington officially refused to comply with the Livingston measure. Ellsworth's report was later found among President Washington's papers. While it is unknown whether the president at any point requested the document directly from the chief justice, Washington relied on the same rationale that the new chief justice had privately offered in his letter. Like Ellsworth, the president cited the House's exclusion from the treaty-making power granted by the Constitution. Also like Ellsworth, Washington emphasized the negative consequences of forcing the president to disclose diplomatic communications. Ellsworth had written Senator Trumbull, "The claim of the House of Representatives to participate in or control the Treaty making power is as unwarranted as it is dangerous." Washington similarly concluded that he could not comply with the resolution "without establishing a dangerous precedent." Future administrations, explained Washington, might resist dispatching diplomatic missions in the first place if they believed that Congress would demand disclosure of the related documents.[13]

Delighted with Washington's message, Federalist congressmen boasted that the president's letter deserved to be transcribed onto white satin and framed for posterity. Democratic-Republican foes of the treaty were less enthused. After Washington refused to budge on the diplomatic documents, they made a final attempt to frustrate the implementation of the Jay Treaty. House opponents argued that they could leverage their chamber's constitutionally granted power over the federal purse to drain the international accord of any required funding. Ellsworth had anticipated this argument in the report he drafted after Livingston's resolution. He wrote that since the power to make treaties was given exclusively to the president with the advice and consent of the Senate, the decision as to whether or not to fund a treaty lay outside of Congress's typical spending powers. Once a valid treaty was made, its funding had to follow as part of the execution of the law. (Along with constitutional provisions and federal statutes, the framers had included treaties in the Constitution's category of "supreme Law," Ellsworth hastened to remind his audience.) The question of treaty appropriations, however, would not vex the Washington administration. The Federalists in the House were able to garner enough votes to defeat the defunding motion by the razor-thin margin of three votes.

FREE-SPEECH CONTROVERSIES

Ellsworth's brief tenure as chief justice lacked any hallmark rulings—with perhaps one notable exception. Whether the federal government could punish seditious speech was the context for Ellsworth's most important ruling as chief justice.

In 1798, two years after Chief Justice Ellsworth assumed his post, Congress passed the Sedition Act, outlawing "any false, scandalous and malicious" writings against the United States government. As in the case of the Jay Treaty, the sedition debate pitted one political camp's preference for principle against the other's allegiance to pragmatism, one's interest in liberty against the other's in order. Although Democratic-Republican leaders believed that the state governments remained free to regulate speech, they were libertarian with respect to federal interference. Instead of granting federal authorities the power to punish antigovernment speech, they trusted that the American people would freely reject subversive speech. During the debate over the sedition bill in the summer of 1798, Congressman Edward Livingston captured his party's position—"let the public judge."[14]

Just as Federalists doubted that the American public could be trusted to direct the nation's external relations, they also rejected the notion that the dangers of seditious speech could be fully avoided absent federal regulation. A free national market in speech could lead to disaster, at least in the near term. Left to themselves, Americans would not respond with sufficient speed or force to those who sought to undermine the national government. Supporters of the Sedition Act maintained that the enemies of the American government were well organized and prepared to act. Congressman Robert Goodloe Harper of South Carolina, a leader of House Federalists, warned of "a treasonable correspondence, carried on by persons in this country with France, of the most criminal nature."[15] Given such a specter, the American people needed more protection than the free market of public opinion could offer.

While the Federalists pushed through Congress a statute that they believed was critical to the protection of national security, Democratic-Republicans earned one important victory. The bill extended to the accused the right of defending speech critical of the federal government on the grounds that the content was true. Under British libel law at the time, a defendant could *not* claim that speech against the government was permissible just because the allegations made in that speech were, in fact, accurate.

Another Democratic-Republican flourish in the Sedition Act was the provision that juries hearing cases brought under the act "shall be judges of the law as well as the fact." In contemporary England, the jury's role was limited to resolving the facts of the case, which, in libel suits, meant determining merely whether the accused made the allegedly libelous statement. Once this factual determination was made, the judge, acting alone, decided whether the statement met the legal definition of libel. Under America's new libel law, however, Congress authorized citizen-jurors not only to resolve factual questions but also to determine whether a party's speech constituted libel under the Sedition Act. Democratic-Republican opponents of the Sedition Act may have lost the war they waged against permitting the federal government to punish antigovernment speech, but they won a significant concession— it would be citizen-jurors, not federal officials, who would decide whether the charged speech violated federal law.

Hard-line Federalists feared that jurors could abuse this power. The libel law, as enacted, placed no limit on the legal determinations that juries were permitted to make. Federalists worried that beyond inquiring into whether the charged speech fell within the prohibitions set forth by the Sedition Act, jurors might ask an additional question: was the Sedition Act itself legal? To answer this, they would have to decide on the constitutionality of federal law. Assuming they found the act to exceed Congress's constitutional authority, citizen-jurors could succeed where Democratic-Republicans in Congress had failed: they could nullify the entire act.

This dispute between Federalists and Democratic-Republicans revealed one of the deepest and most enduring fault lines in the nation's political life. Whereas opponents of the Sedition Act looked to incorporate citizen-jurors and state governments to ease the law's application, Federalists believed that allowing civilian jurors to declare the law unconstitutional upset the structure that the Constitution had created for the federal government. Giving citizen-jurors the power to judge the legality of the Sedition Act, objected Federalist congressman James A. Bayard of Delaware, was to "put it into the power of a jury to declare [the Sedition Act] an unconstitutional law, instead of leaving this to be determined where it ought to be determined, by the Judiciary."[16] Fundamentally, the dispute centered on the question of whether those outside the federal government could prevent the enforcement of federal law.

As chief justice, Ellsworth had the opportunity to respond to the two questions raised by the Sedition Act: First, was the act itself legal? And second, should federal officials be the sole arbiters of the legality of their acts? Ellsworth answered the first question affirmatively. He recognized the existence of federal common law, which, in his view, justified Congress in enacting a statute that protected the national government. Ellsworth's response to the second question was related to the first. He believed that by calling on citizen-jurors to apply federal common law, national security could be enhanced without sacrificing locally protected liberties.

Ellsworth set forth his arguments in a charge delivered to a South Carolina grand jury empaneled on May 7, 1799. At the time, Supreme Court justices interacted regularly with civilian jurors, since, under Ellsworth's Judiciary Act, they traveled throughout the states to hear cases brought in circuit courts. Jury instructions were one of the tools that Supreme Court justices used to inform the public of their own perspectives on pending legal questions. Addressing the South Carolina jury, Ellsworth explained that a "residue" of authority—separate and apart from the provisions found in federal statutes—allowed the federal government to punish "offences against the United States." Delineating the implications of this conviction, the chief justice chose his words carefully. He did not maintain that federal officials had broad authority to arrest individuals on the grounds that they posed a vague threat to the federal government. The "residue" of federal authority extended only to "acts contravening the laws of nations"—a category of cases that juries would "rarely meet with"—as well as any "acts manifestly subversive of the national government, or some of its powers specified in the constitution." Ellsworth was careful to emphasize that the federal government's general, nonstatutory authority to prosecute individuals for disloyal conduct did not extend far. "Manifestly subversive," he stressed, meant "to confine criminality to [cases of] clearness and certainty." The federal government could not bring nonstatutory suits where the allegedly subversive conduct was of "doubtful tendency."[17]

Significantly, Ellsworth also instructed the South Carolina grand jury to keep in view the vast legal forest in which the Constitution was planted. The forest was Anglo-American common law, "the maxims and principles" that were, in Ellsworth's words, "brought from the country of our ancestors" and adopted as "the law of every part of the union at the formation of the national compact." Ellsworth's belief that the common law remained in effect was relevant because sedition was a crime under this body of law. According to Blackstone's *Commentaries*, the standard compilation of the common law that guided the legal analysis of many early American lawyers and judges (Ellsworth among them), "false and pretended prophecies, with intent to disturb the peace, [were] equally unlawful."[18] From the chief justice's perspective, the framers of the Constitution (Ellsworth again among them) never intended for the Constitution to replace the common law. "So pregnant with mischief," railed Ellsworth, "is a supposition irreconcilable with those frequent references in the constitution, to the common law, as a living code." Ellsworth implored the jurors to use the principles of the common law in order to determine "what acts are misdemeanors." For the chief justice, the common law was no collection of vague standards, but "the rules then, of a known law, matured by the reason of ages, and which Americans have ever been tenacious as a birth-right." And under the common law, as Ellsworth reminded the civil jurors, "conduct, therefore, clearly destructive of a government, or its powers, which the people have ordained to *exist*, must be criminal."[19]

Ellsworth's conclusion that federal prosecution for seditious speech was justified under the common law aligned him with Federalist politicians. But his answer to the second question raised by the law cut in favor of the act's critics. While Ellsworth believed that the Sedition Act was legitimate, he also asserted that citizen-jurors were under no obligation to enforce congressional statutes that they found in violation of the "national compact." The "obligation of the citizen to obey or of the magistrate to execute" a law, he declared, extended only until the lawmakers "overleap the constitution." In this rare case, the fundamental duty of the juror was to protect the "national compact," not the written law. To be sure, these miniature public councils would not be without guidance. They would perform their task aided by the majestic rules that they had inherited in the common law. Nevertheless, Ellsworth was willing to share with civilian jurors the power of analyzing a federal statute's constitutionality. According to legal scholar William R. Casto, Ellsworth "saw the grand jury process itself as a procedural limit to common-law prosecutions."[20]

Ellsworth's conviction that civilian jurors, standing on constitutional grounds, could prevent a prosecution based on a validly enacted federal statute was not shared by his Federalist colleagues, who preferred to consolidate the power of reviewing a statute's constitutionality in judicial hands. "The Judicial powers," read one of Justice Samuel Chase's charges, "are the only proper and competent authority to decide whether any Law made by Congress, or any of the State Legislatures is contrary to or in violation of the *federal* Constitution." Even the more moderate Justice William Paterson, who had crafted the compromise provisions of the Judiciary Act in the Senate a decade earlier, charged jurors to "have nothing to do with the constitutionality or unconstitutionality of the sedition law," adding that "Congress has said that the author and publisher of seditious libels is to be punished and until the law is declared null and void by a tribunal competent for the purpose, its validity cannot be disputed."[21]

The ennobling role that Ellsworth afforded to civilian jurors was not lost upon Democratic-Republican critics of the Sedition Act. The South Carolina grand jury "returned their acknowledgments" for the chief justice's "excellent charge," and requested that the instructions be published. Roughly one dozen papers around the nation accepted the offer. Two months later, a negative assessment of Ellsworth's instructions appeared in the Democratic-Republican *Virginia Argus*. However, the author paid due respect to Ellsworth's judiciousness. "Your charge to the grand jury for the district of South Carolina," began the five-page discourse, "proves you to be a man superior to most of your brethren. . . . Greatly to your honor you have avoided an interference with political subjects; you have not imitated the too frequent example of disgracing the bench of justice, by passionate and indecent invectives against your fellow citizens, and against foreigners; and above all you have not violated that sacred principle of our constitution" separating the judicial from the executive and legislative branches.[22]

In a day when Federalist judges and many of the party's officials elsewhere were prone to political pessimism, Ellsworth's measured pronouncements offered a calmer exposition of Federalist principles. Had his example been widely followed, it might have kept his party from meeting its electoral demise in the decade that followed. But beyond the careful language, the substance of Ellsworth's support of federal common law was also neatly balanced, containing elements of both the Anti-Federalist and Federalist political canons. Like the Anti-Federalists, Ellsworth had shown himself comfortable with granting citizen-jurors a significant role in federal judicial proceedings, even to the point of permitting them to nullify a federal law that they found to be unconstitutional. But the Federalist Ellsworth insisted that federal common law existed, which presupposed—contrary to Anti-Federalist ideology—that at a certain point the citizens of all the separate states had consented to adopt a general body of principles that would guide the federal government's actions and, crucially, empower its officials to protect the nation.

Ellsworth's case for the federal common law was consistent with his general approach throughout his political career. He sought civic harmony in the proper balance between central authority and local autonomy. His jurisprudence offered something to his era's proponents of national security *and* to defenders of democratic civil liberties: the recognition of federal common law allowed federal officials to exercise the powers necessary to protect the national government, while the incorporation of the jury ensured that these same common-law principles were applied fairly. Taken together, the separate parts of Ellsworth's judicial approach gracefully bridged a gulf between the dominant currents of the nation's political life, combining the democratic spirit of the Anti-Federalists with the practical-minded nationalism of the Federalists. The chief justice showed how the survival of America's "national compact" could occur because of, not in spite of, the American people.

ELLSWORTH'S FINAL ACT

In March 1797, Americans witnessed the first change of presidential administrations. The transfer of power from George Washington to John Adams occurred seamlessly, with Ellsworth playing a role in the ceremony. Elevated to the high court one year earlier, he became the first chief justice to administer the oath of office to an incoming president. It was fitting as well as historic that circumstance placed Ellsworth next to John Adams on the new president's inauguration day. The pair had much in common. Like Ellsworth, Adams was a New England–born lawyer whose father sent him to college to become a minister. Politically, Ellsworth and Adams were independent-minded Federalists. That is, they believed that the federal government should be strong, but not excessively centralized; that the ruled as well as their rulers needed to be checked; and that George Washington exemplified their party's spirit.

The defining diplomatic issue of the Adams administration would bring the chief justice and the president into their closest collaboration. Two years after his inauguration, Adams dispatched Ellsworth to negotiate a peaceful solution to a maritime war with France. This diplomatic mission—Ellsworth's first—was also his final act in national politics.

"My entrance into office," Adams remarked during his first month as president, "is marked by a misunderstanding with France." Less than two weeks after taking the oath, President Adams learned that the French government had refused to accept President Washington's appointed envoy, the former Constitutional Convention delegate Charles Cotesworth Pinckney. Aggravating this diplomatic slight, reports circulated that the French were taking an aggressive posture toward American commerce.

Over a twelve-month period beginning in 1796, French vessels seized more than three hundred American ships. France's policy was a response to the Jay Treaty. America and France had been allied by a 1778 accord, but the French interpreted America's recent treaty with Great Britain as severing France's wartime alliance with the United States. According to Alexander DeConde, the twentieth-century diplomatic historian and author of the classic text on the Adams-era conflict, *The Quasi-War: The Politics and Diplomacy of the Undeclared War with France, 1797–1801*, the Franco-American fallout "dwarfed all else in the administration of John Adams."[23]

Despite the hardening of relations and his own decided lack of enthusiasm for the French Revolution, President Adams was determined to avert war with France. At a pre-inaugural meeting with Vice President Thomas Jefferson, Adams had suggested dispatching a three-person commission for a special mission to France. To join Pinckney, a South Carolina Federalist, the president hoped to send former congressman Elbridge Gerry of Massachusetts and Congressman James Madison of Virginia. Offering a politically and geographically mixed delegation—neither Gerry nor Madison was a Federalist—was characteristic of Adams's moderation. Despite the report that the French government's chilly reception had driven Pinckney to Amsterdam, Adams remained committed to his plan. In the summer of 1797, the administration dispatched Gerry and future chief justice John Marshall (who took Madison's place when the Virginia representative refused the offer) to resolve the rising Franco-American tensions.

If designed to prevent war, Adams's conciliatory effort failed. In fact, it catapulted the United States closer to armed conflict with France. In April 1798, the president disclosed to Congress the treatment that the commissioners had received. As a precondition of negotiation, France's foreign minister, the famed Charles-Maurice de Talleyrand-Périgord, attempted through three intermediaries to elicit a bribe from the Americans. President Adams kept the identity of the three French agents secret, labeling them as "X," "Y," and "Z" when he consulted with Congress. The revelation of the XYZ Affair, as it was later called, generated a popular tide for reprisal, as Americans regarded the mistreatment of the administration's diplomats to be an affront to the nation's honor. An independent republic should not have to pay to negotiate with an equal sovereign. "Millions for defense, but not one cent for tribute!" cried outraged Americans. Public support for President Adams rose.[24]

Federalist Party insiders, who believed that the time to "preach peace" had passed, hoped to capitalize on the public's new hawkishness. Beginning in the spring of 1798, congressional Federalists passed a series of measures to bolster the nation's security and defense.

At a time when the nation's forces stood at less than four thousand, Congress authorized plans for a "provisional army" of 25,000, before reducing the number to 10,000. Federalists pushed through the Alien and Sedition Acts during the same legislative session. While leading to the enactment of various Federalist policies, the escalating tensions with France highlighted a widening rift in Ellsworth's party. Adams, a long-standing opponent of "standing armies," had wished for a more modest buildup of troops from Congress. The president also stopped short of pushing for a war declaration. In December 1798, Adams informed Congress that he would resume negotiations with France "at her option." If France would receive another envoy, Adams was not averse to resolving the Quasi-War at the bargaining table.[25]

Three months later, President Adams acted. Since the crisis began, Adams had followed developments in France from the dispatches that he received from American officials, including his son John Quincy, serving on the European continent. The reports indicated that France was now willing to discuss a rapprochement. Satisfied that France had met the required conditions for diplomatic talks, Adams sent word to Congress, requesting the Senate's approval for his nomination of William Vans Murray as the U.S. minister to France. Murray, a former Federalist congressman from Maryland, was serving as the U.S. minister to the Netherlands. The decision to negotiate with France—regardless of the emissary chosen for the assignment—was itself controversial. "Of all the brave acts of his career—his defense of the British soldiers in the Boston Massacre trials, the signing of the Declaration of Independence, his crossing of the Atlantic in the winter of 1778, the high risk of his mission to Holland," writes historian David McCullough, the "brief message sent to the United States Senate" requesting the approval of a new minister "was perhaps the bravest."[26]

The nomination stunned Congress, bringing its legislative session to a halt. An observer reported that day that House Federalists "acted as if struck by a thunderbolt." The orator [Congressman Harrison Gray] Otis, the friend and confidant of Adams, showed embarrassment, grew pale. The House adjourned, and is still adjourned today."[27]

Throughout his presidency, Adams had maintained a distance from Federalists who demanded a more hawkish federal reaction to the crisis with France. The Murray nomination had widened the breach into an open feud. "There is not a Sound mind from Maine to Georgia that has not been shocked by it," opined one Boston

Federalist. Adams's secretary of state, Timothy Pickering, agreed. The "*honor* of the country is prostrated in the dust," he wrote. "God grant that its safety not be in jeopardy."[28]

Less than a week after the nomination, five Federalist senators met with President Adams to insist that he withdraw the plan to dispatch Murray on a peace mission. The conference was not the first time that Federalist insiders had sought to persuade a president to adopt their course for conducting foreign policy.

Five years earlier, in March 1794, Oliver Ellsworth had brought to President Washington the solution of the Friends of Peace for settling America's tense relations with Great Britain. On both occasions, a group of Federalist senators had attempted to influence the president. But the Friends of Peace had suggested an envoy to avert war with Britain. The Federalist senators that met with President Adams called themselves "friends of order," not peace.[29]

The meeting between the Federalist senators and Adams failed to produce a compromise between the parties. The senators offered to support talks with France provided that the administration bolster the mission with two additional envoys. But Adams refused. "I have on mature reflection," he told the senators, "made up my mind, and I will neither withdraw nor modify the nomination." Regrouping the following evening, Senate Federalists agreed to reject the Murray nomination when it came to a vote.[30]

Before the Murray nomination came to a head in the Senate, Chief Justice Ellsworth discussed the matter with President Adams. During their meeting, Ellsworth managed to succeed where the Federalist senators had not, convincing Adams to appoint the extra envoys "so as to embrace more of the confidence of the country."[31]

Ellsworth's role expanded when Adams refused to appoint as the additional envoys Alexander Hamilton and former Massachusetts senator George Cabot, the trusted Federalists the senators had recommended. Instead, Adams proposed Ellsworth himself and Patrick Henry of Virginia to round out the committee of three. The Senate promptly approved the slate. When the Virginian declined to serve due to his age, Ellsworth recommended Henry's replacement—North Carolina governor William R. Davie, a southern Federalist in the moderate mold of Adams and Ellsworth.[32]

Although it quelled an open party feud, the enlarged mission did not entirely assuage Federalist hawks. Fisher Ames of Massachusetts lamented that most Federalists still opposed negotiation even if they supported Adams's proposed negotiators. "Peace with France they think an evil," he wrote, "and holding out the hope of it another, as it tends to chill the public fervor."[33]

These hard-liners pleaded with Ellsworth to petition the president to drop the peace mission. But Ellsworth refused to counsel Adams accordingly. As Secretary of State Pickering correctly observed, Ellsworth felt duty bound to accept the appointment. "This excellent man," he wrote of the chief justice, "when he was here in August, saw no alternative *but he must go.*" In a September 1799 letter to Adams, Ellsworth reiterated that whether he would sail to France was a decision that lay ultimately with the president. "It is, Sir," Ellsworth closed the dispatch, "my duty to obey, not advise." The following month, Adams visited Ellsworth at his home in Connecticut. Once again, the chief justice spoke of duty. In Adams's words, "On my way I called upon Chief Justice Ellsworth, at his seat in Windsor, and had a conversation of perhaps two hours with him. He was perfectly candid. Whatever should be the determination, he was ready at an hour's warning to comply."[34]

Other Federalists, however, still hoped to change the president's mind. In October 1799, a crucial meeting was arranged in

Trenton, the temporary capital of the United States, as a result of a yellow fever threat in Philadelphia. The summit brought together the president, his cabinet, Alexander Hamilton, and Ellsworth, who had only recently met with Adams at the chief justice's Windsor home. Surveying the attendees, the president asked "whether Ellsworth and Hamilton had come all the way from Windsor and New York to persuade me to countermand the mission." Ellsworth did not, though he did counsel Adams to postpone the mission. As Adams recorded it, at a private dinner "Mr. Ellsworth expressed an opinion somewhat similar to that of the Heads of Departments," that is, for postponement. The steadfast Adams countered with his reasons for immediately dispatching the envoys, and managed, from his perspective, to sway the chief justice. "The result of the conversation," Adams concluded, "was that Mr. Ellsworth declared himself satisfied, and willing to embark as soon as I pleased." Two weeks later, Ellsworth left for Paris.[35]

Adams's selection of Ellsworth was reminiscent of Washington's selection of Chief Justice John Jay to serve as the negotiator of the 1794 treaty with Britain, as well as Congress's selection of Adams himself to serve as a European diplomat during the Revolutionary War. The Adams, Jay, and Ellsworth line of foreign emissaries represents, in historian Jack Rakove's estimation, an "essential aspect of the American diplomatic tradition: the belief that the conduct of foreign relations is properly the province not of grand strategic thinkers but of lawyers, with their ingrained concern to ensure that contracts are enforced, contingencies foreseen, and rules laid down to adjudicate all disputes."[36]

"Appearances Are Strong in Favor of a General Peace"

Before departing from Newport, the beautiful seaport of the state whose earlier Anti-Federalist policies had prompted Ellsworth's invective, Oliver wrote Abigail a farewell missive: "I pray to God to preserve us & you & the dear children I leave with you and in due time to bring us to rejoice together again." Landing at Lisbon, Ellsworth notified Abigail that he and Oliver Jr. had completed their transatlantic voyage "after a rough passage of twenty-four days in which I suffered too much for my patience," referring likely to the gout that now afflicted the fifty-four-year-old Ellsworth. From Portugal, the Ellsworth father and son team braved "so bad a state of roads" (in the elder Oliver's words), traveling by land through northern Spain to Paris. When they finally arrived in the French capital in March 1800, the diplomat was understandably relieved to have completed the arduous trek of "six thousand miles of storms . . . and another thousand of mountains & mud." Ellsworth was pleased to report that he was at last beginning "to repair" after "four months fatigue."[37]

When the talks finally began, the American commissioners presented their objectives as twofold: to secure reparations for American cargo seized by French vessels since the beginning of hostilities, and to reach a new treaty with France that abrogated the terms of the 1778 alliance. In reply, the French negotiators offered a choice: either France would reimburse the damages sought by the United States on the condition that terms of the earlier alliance were renewed, or it would consent to undo the earlier alliance without guaranteeing the payment of damages.

At a standstill with their counterparts, Ellsworth and his fellow commissioners made a crucial decision to sacrifice one of their two objectives. They agreed to drop their demand that France reimburse the United States for the entirety of the property it had seized. They were willing to accept France's pledge to return only the captured cargo that it had not yet condemned. At the same time, the American counteroffer bound the French to "abstain from all unfriendly acts" against American commerce, while also lifting the obligations that the United States owed France under the earlier agreements between the two nations. The French promptly agreed to these terms.

Although President Adams delivered the proposed settlement to the Senate in December 1800, one month after he was defeated for reelection by Thomas Jefferson, preoccupation with the Electoral College contest between Jefferson and Aaron Burr kept lawmakers from acting on it until the following month. On its arrival, the treaty triggered the predictable responses. To Federalist hawks, the treaty marked "another chapter in the book of humiliation." In particular, the enraged hard-liners from Ellsworth's own party directed their ire at him. The chief justice's presence on the commission had once been a source of consolation for them. "I rely on Mr. E. as much as any man can," Fisher Ames had written a year earlier, "to watch the foe, and to parry the stroke of her dagger." But the same Federalists soon questioned Ellsworth's physical and mental health. Theodore Sedgwick pronounced that the "mind as well as body of Mr. Ellsworth are rendered feeble by disease." In a letter to Hamilton of December 25, 1800, Oliver Wolcott Jr. concluded, "You will be afflicted on reading the treaty with France. Mr. Ellsworth's health is, I fear, destroyed."[38]

Moderates within Adams's party, on the other hand, took a positive view. "I am pleased with the Convention," wrote former

South Carolina congressman William Smith, then serving as the U.S. minister to Portugal, adding that "all the great points concerning navigation are settled to our advantage." Meanwhile, Democratic-Republican leaders signaled their willingness to support the settlement.

On January 23, 1801, the Senate approved the treaty by a vote of sixteen to fourteen, or four votes shy of the two-thirds majority required for ratification. President Adams resubmitted the treaty. Alexander DeConde concludes that the eventual reversal was due to the growing Federalist awareness of the public's support for the settlement. Leading merchants, in particular, believed that the agreement would secure avenues for valuable international commerce.[39] On February 3, 1801, the Senate ratified the agreement by a vote of twenty-two to nine.[40] In retrospect, William Vans Murray, one of Ellsworth's fellow commissioners, regretted that the settlement had not arrived in the United States before the electorate submitted its ballots in November 1800. Had it arrived earlier, Murray speculated, "its influence [would] have been auxiliary" to President Adams's bid for reelection.[41]

Although the former chief justice had complained of his health, he remained mentally acute throughout the trip. In November 1800, following the treaty talks, his conegotiator Murray wrote that Ellsworth had "a head of iron—just iron—that works with the precision of a mill, without its quickness and giddy manner. I profoundly admire the neatness and accuracy of his mind."[42] Ellsworth's account of the treaty negotiation shows that he understood exactly the trade offs that he was willing to make in order to reach a harmonious accord with France. "My best efforts, and those of my colleagues," Ellsworth acknowledged to Timothy Pickering, "have not obtained all that justice required, or which the policy of

France should have given." But the agreement was justified because it avoided a potentially devastating conflict with France. "Enough is, however, done," he continued to Pickering, "to extricate the United States from a contest, which it might be as difficult to relinquish with honor, as to pursue with a prospect of advantage." The chief justice explained that he had based his willingness to settle the existing disputes with the French on an assessment that proved accurate. Peace between the nations was possible. In contrast to Federalist hawks, Ellsworth believed, as he wrote to Oliver Wolcott Jr., that "the reign of Jacobinism is over in France, and appearances are strong in favor of a general peace." Sure enough, in the wake of the settlement, the French government maintained an amicable posture toward the United States. In 1803, when France agreed to the Louisiana Purchase, Napoleon would describe the transaction as characteristic of the recently improved relationship between France and the United States.[43]

A "Most Meritorious" Finale

Considering the alternatives to the peace settlement with France, and its ultimate outcome, DeConde concludes his study of the Quasi-War with high praise for the diplomatic mission: "From the perspective of a century and three quarters it seems fair to conclude that perhaps no peace settlement has brought the nation greater benefits for so little cost." While praising the French for their willingness to negotiate, DeConde singled out Ellsworth and his fellow commissioners as deserving credit for their "patient diplomacy."[44]

As a first-time diplomat, Ellsworth may have been unfamiliar with the niceties of this new assignment. But on the important decision as to whether to negotiate a reasonable peace, the chief justice drew upon considerable experience. For the previous two decades, he had labored to preserve American independence from imprudent partisanship, seeking to find the harmonious consensus amid the threats to America's unity. From his time as a Revolutionary congressman to his return to Philadelphia as a Constitutional Convention delegate, from his defense of the Constitution to his crafting of the Judiciary Act, from his advocacy of the Jay Treaty to his support for federal common law as chief justice, Oliver Ellsworth had understood that the critical questions of national independence and domestic harmony required a carefully measured approach.

In his final assignment, Ellsworth followed dutifully the president's intention to secure peace with France. For this, Ellsworth earned the lasting esteem of President Adams, who proudly looked back on Ellsworth's final assignment. "I will defend my missions to France," Adams later wrote, "as long as I have an eye to direct my hand or a finger to hold my pen. They were the most disinterested and meritorious actions of my life. I reflect upon them with so much satisfaction, that I desire no other inscription over my gravestone than: 'Here lies John Adams, who took upon himself the responsibility of the peace with France in the year 1800.'"[45]

The chief justice's mission had resulted in a lasting peace—a fitting conclusion indeed to this practical statesman's federal service.

AFTERWORD

AFTER THE TREATY NEGOTIATIONS WITH FRANCE, OLIVER ELLS-
worth sent home his resignation as chief justice of the United States
on October 16, 1800, from the port city of Le Havre on France's Nor-
mandy coast. Four years earlier, Ellsworth had felt obliged to leave
the Senate for a seat on the Supreme Court. Later, he responded to
Adams's call to diplomatic service. His final words to Adams from
Europe again displayed the Connecticut statesman's sense of duty. "I
have the honour to be, Sir," he closed, "with very great respect, Your
most obedient Oliver Ellsworth."[1] Although Ellsworth's retirement
did not permit a formal farewell, it came at a fitting moment. Ellsworth had for two decades labored with intelligence and wisdom
toward the goal of protecting national unity and achieving benefi-
cial compromises. Having performed one final useful task across the
ocean, he left the service of the United States government.

Thomas Jefferson had been elected president in 1800, ushering
in the first Democratic-Republican administration. Ellsworth fol-

lowed the political developments from abroad. At the conclusion of the negotiations with France, he traveled to England, where he learned of Jefferson's election. In 1800, Ellsworth had remarked "that there is in a government like ours a natural antipathy to system of every kind." The victory of the Democratic-Republican standard-bearer further convinced Ellsworth that the prospects for a strong national government were dim.[2]

Coupled with "the gravel and the gout" that he complained of in his resignation letter, Ellsworth's concern over the direction of national politics likely played a role in his decision to retire from the Supreme Court. If distressed, however, Ellsworth did not despair. The change in administrations, he reasoned, would allow "good men" to "get a breathing spell." As for the new incumbents, Ellsworth doubted that they would be able to "run the ship aground." He wisely described the challenge that faced Jefferson's traditionally Anti-Federalist supporters now that they were in power. Jefferson's "party," he wrote his friend Rufus King from Bath, England, in January 1801, "must support the government while he administers it; and if others are consistent, and do the same, the government may even be consolidated, and acquire new confidence."[3]

By retiring as chief justice when he did, Oliver Ellsworth contributed indirectly to the consolidation of the federal government's power. His resignation reached the capital in time for outgoing president John Adams to select Ellsworth's replacement. Adams turned to another moderate Federalist, his recently appointed secretary of state, John Marshall. It would be more than thirty years before another president would have the opportunity to nominate a chief justice. Through his opinions, Marshall advanced the Federalist philosophy even while the political branches of the federal government were under Democratic-Republican control.

In 1801, Ellsworth finally returned to "his beautiful mansion in Windsor." Although retired from national politics, the former chief justice remained active. He completed his political career where it had begun. A year after returning to Connecticut, he was elected to the upper house of the state legislature in time to weigh in on the Baptist Petition controversy.

For Ellsworth, politics had always been a matter of addressing solvable problems. These tended to be those that were closest to home. During his retirement, he distinguished himself from many of his Federalist associates, who passed their exiles fixated on national politics. "Always writing, writing, writing," protested Ellsworth of Fisher Ames.[4]

Ellsworth found it more fruitful to focus on his native state. Apart from his political duties, he ran a general store that he owned and operated with two of his sons. In 1804, he became the *Connecticut Courant*'s regular agricultural columnist. During his sojourn in England, he had acquired several books on the subject and now sought to transmit his knowledge to his state's farmers.[5]

Ellsworth's involvement in state government permitted him to advance his political principles at that level. In 1802, he made a notable contribution when the General Assembly selected him to chair a committee appointed to consider a petition by Connecticut's growing Baptist minority to end the religious subsidies that Connecticut's residents were required to pay. At the time, the established church of Connecticut was Congregationalism—the faith to which Ellsworth remained devoted. Under state law, Congregationalist churches received a sum for the salaries of their ministers and other religious costs, paid by the state's residents. By the end of the eighteenth century, members of three specified religious denominations (Baptists, Quakers, and Anglicans) were permitted to direct their contributions to their own churches. However, to qualify for this exemption, it was necessary to show actual attendance at a church belonging to one of the three exempted denominations. Proponents of the Baptist Petition objected to this arrangement; they sought to prevent those not affiliated with a particular church from having to pay for its activities. The most famous consequence of the Baptist Petition was the response that it elicited from President Thomas Jefferson, who replied to the solicitation of support from a committee of Baptists from Danbury, Connecticut, with a letter that included his famous claim that in declaring "that their legislature should 'make no law respecting an establishment of religion, or prohibiting the free exercise thereof,'" the American people had built "a wall of separation between Church & State."

Ellsworth's response to the Baptist Petition ran in the other direction. During the inaugural gathering of the Assembly's select committee, Ellsworth reportedly tossed a copy of the petition on the floor and, after putting his foot on top of it, remarked, "This is where it belongs."[6] After a week of deliberation, Ellsworth authored the committee's formal statement opposing the petition. Ellsworth's opinion, which appeared in the *Connecticut Courant* on June 7, 1802, restated the basic view that government was based upon the will of the majority. The necessary acts of providing for the general welfare required, therefore, that all individuals support certain programs even if they did not directly use them. "The right of the legislature to oblige each individual of the community to contribute toward the support of schools for the instruction of children, or of the courts of justice for the protection of rights is not questioned." Nor was it problematic, he continued, for the community to require an individual to pay for these public services "because he has no children to be instructed, no injuries to be redressed, or because he conscientiously believes those institutions useless."[7]

Ellsworth linked the work of churches to the health of the community. "The primary objects of government," he stated, "are the peace, order, and prosperity of society." For citizens to obtain these objectives, the former chief justice continued, "good morals are essential." He went on to assert that religious institutions could be "eminently useful and important" to republican societies and therefore the proper recipients of public aid. Ellsworth assumed that religious institutions would instill values that supported the goals of peace and prosperity, just as New Divinity Calvinism had given him a worldview that shaped his political thought, making him into the cautious and prudent leader that he was. "In the opinion of the committee," Ellsworth closed, "the legislature may aid the maintenance of that religion whose benign influence on morals is universally acknowledged."[8]

In 1807, after years of continuing to fulfill duties that his peers assigned him, Ellsworth was finally forced to turn down an assignment. Connecticut's legislature appointed Ellsworth to serve as chief justice in the state's recently reshuffled judiciary. Although he initially accepted the post, Ellsworth later declined, citing his deteriorating health. On November 26, 1807, Oliver Ellsworth died in his Windsor home at the age of sixty-three.

Inside this home lay a statement that Ellsworth had written. "I have visited several countries," it read, "and I like my own the best. I have been in all the states of the Union, and Connecticut is the best state. Windsor is the pleasantest town in the state of Connecticut, and I have the pleasantest place in the town of Windsor. I am content, perfectly content, to die on the banks of the Connecticut."[9]

The Connecticut statesman had his wish granted. His life of public service had come to an end in the "pleasantest place" that he knew, in the federal republic that he helped shape.

NOTES

<hr />

Preface

1. William G. Brown, *The Life of Oliver Ellsworth* (New York: Macmillan, 1905), 225.

2. Thomas P. Slaughter, *The Whiskey Rebellion: Frontier Epilogue to the American Revolution* (New York: Oxford University Press, 1986), 4.

Chapter 1: The Education of a Puritan Politician

1. David M. Roth, *Connecticut: A Bicentennial History* (New York: W. W. Norton, 1979), 34.

2. Christopher Collier, *All Politics is Local: Family, Friends, and Provincial Interests in the Creation of the Constitution* (Lebanon, NH: University Press of New England, 2003), 13–14.

3. Albert E. Van Dusen, *Connecticut* (New York: Random House, 1961), 19–23.

4. Alden T. Vaughan, ed., *The Puritan Tradition in America* 1620–1730 (Columbia, SC: University of South Carolina Press, 1972), xii.

5. Forrest McDonald, *We the People: The Economic Origins of the Constitution* (New Brunswick, NJ: Transaction Press, 1992), 415–16.

6. Vaughan, *The Puritan Tradition in America 1620–1730*, 3–9.

7. Van Dusen, *Connecticut*, 11, 23, 41.

8. Roth, *Connecticut: A Bicentennial History*, 40–41.

9. Freeman W. Meyer, *Connecticut Congregationalism in the Revolutionary Era* (Hartford, CT: The American Revolution Bicentennial Commission of Connecticut, 1977), 7.

10. Charles W. Elliot, ed., *American Historical Documents 1000–1904* (New York: P. F. Collier & Son, 1910), 63–69.

11. Meyer, *Connecticut Congregationalism in the Revolutionary Era*, 15.

12. Elliot, *American Historical Documents 1000–1904*, 66.

13. Van Dusen, *Connecticut*, 70.

14. Roth, *Connecticut: A Bicentennial History*, 41.

15. Collier, *All Politics is Local: Family, Friends, and Provincial Interests in the Creation of the Constitution*, 18.

16. Ibid.

17. Reverend Joseph Bellamy, *The Works of Joseph Bellamy, D.D.*, vol. 1, (Boston: Doctrinal Tract and Book Society, 1853), 588.

18. Julia Baldini, "A Look Back: The 1910 Census," *Windsor Historical Society News* 28, no. 1 (March 2010): 1.

19. Brown, *The Life of Oliver Ellsworth*, 9–10.

20. Henry R. Stiles, *A Supplement to the History and Genealogies of Ancient Windsor, Conn.* (Albany, NY: J. Munsell, 1863), 58.

21. Harold E. Selesky, *War and Society in Colonial Connecticut* (New Haven, CT: Yale University Press, 1990), 76; Brown, *The Life of Oliver Ellsworth*, 11.

22. Roth, *Connecticut: A Bicentennial History*, 62.

23. Elizabeth C. Barney Buel, "Oliver Ellsworth," *New England Magazine* (July 1904): 611–26; Brown, *The Life of Oliver Ellsworth*, 11–12.

24. Brown, *The Life of Oliver Ellsworth*, 11.

25. William R. Casto, *Oliver Ellsworth and the Creation of the Federal Republic* (New York: Second Circuit Committee on History and Commemorative Events, 1997), 5.

26. Brown, *The Life of Oliver Ellsworth*, 12n1.

27. Casto, *Oliver Ellsworth and the Creation of the Federal Republic*, 5–7; Henry R. Stiles, *History of Ancient Windsor, Connecticut* (New York: Charles R. Norton, 1859), 360.

28. Casto, *Oliver Ellsworth and the Creation of the Federal Republic*, 7.

29. Stiles, *History of Ancient Windsor, Connecticut*, 360.

30. Casto, *Oliver Ellsworth and the Creation of the Federal Republic*, 8.

31. Ibid., 9.

32. Ibid., 9–12.

33. Ibid., 9.

34. Reverend Joseph Bellamy, *Four Sermons on the Wisdom of God in the Permission of Sins* (Morristown, NJ: Henry P. Russell, 1804), 36–38, 42, 46, 51, 54, 91.

35. Ibid., 36.

36. Ibid., 23.

37. Ibid., 28.

38. Ibid., 108 (italics in original).

39. Casto, *Oliver Ellsworth and the Creation of the Federal Republic*, 12.

40. Missionary Society of Connecticut, *A Summary of Christian Doctrine and Practice: Designed Especially for the Use of the People in the New Settlements of the United States of America* (Hartford, CT: Hudson & Goodwin, 1804), ch. 8, 14.

41. Bellamy, *The Works of Joseph Bellamy, D.D.*, 1.:579.

42. Ibid., 589.

43. William C. Placher, *Readings in the History of Christian Theology, From the Reformation to the Present, vol. 2* (Philadelphia: Westminster Press, n.d.), 109.

44. Bellamy, *The Works of Joseph Bellamy, D.D.*, 1:589.

45. Ibid.

46. Paul Leicester Ford, *Essays on the Constitution of the United States* (Brooklyn: Historical Printing Club, 1892), 199.

47. Paul H. Smith, ed., *Letters of Delegates to Congress 1774–1789*, vol 2, (Washington, D.C.: Government Printing Office, 1976–1996), 487–90.

48. Jonathan Elliot, ed., *The Debates in the Several State Conventions on the Adoption of the Federal Constitution*, vol. 2, (Washington, D.C.: Library of Congress, 1836), 185.

49. Oliver Ellsworth, "Charge to the Grand Jury of the Circuit Court for the District of Georgia," April 26, 1796, in Maeva Marcus, ed., *Documentary History of the Supreme Court of the United States 1789–1800*, vol. 3, (New York: Columbia University, 1992), 119.

50. Missionary Society of Connecticut, *A Summary of Christian Doctrine*, ch. 20.

Chapter 2: Revolutionary Lessons

1. Roth, *Connecticut: A Bicentennial History*, 58–59.

2. Casto, *Oliver Ellsworth and the Creation of the Federal Republic*, 14.

3. Ibid.

4. Brown, *The Life of Oliver Ellsworth*, 16.

5. Casto, *Oliver Ellsworth and the Creation of the Federal Republic*, 15.

6. Ibid.

7. Brown, *The Life of Oliver Ellsworth*, 18.

8. Ibid., 19.

9. Ibid., 20–21.

10. Ibid., 327–28. For the letter to Abigail, see Mary Philotheta Root, ed., *Character Sketches, Connecticut Daughters of the American Revolution* (New Haven, CT: Tuttle, Morehouse, & Taylor Co., 1901), 87–88.

11. Brown, *The Life of Oliver Ellsworth*, 285.

12. Richard John Lettieri, *Connecticut's Young Man of the Revolution: Oliver Ellsworth* (Hartford, CT: American Revolution Bicentennial Commission of Connecticut, 1978), 13.

13. Root, *Character Sketches, Connecticut Daughters of the American Revolution*, 79; Lettieri, *Connecticut's Young Man of the Revolution: Oliver Ellsworth*, 14.

14. Lettieri, *Connecticut's Young Man of the Revolution: Oliver Ellsworth*, 13.

15. Brown, *The Life of Oliver Ellsworth*, 25.

16. Ibid., 28; Henry Flanders, *The Lives and Times of the Chief Justices of the Supreme Court of the United States*, vol. 2, (1855; repr., Buffalo, NY: William S. Hein & Co, 2004), 66.

17. James H. Hudson, ed., *Supplement to Max Farrand's The Records of the Federal Convention of 1787* (New Haven, CT: Yale University Press, 1987), 177–78.

18. Smith, *Letters of Delegates to Congress 1774–1789*, 20:191.

19. Oliver Ellsworth to Abigail Ellsworth, March 8, 1789, Ellsworth Papers, (Hartford, CT: Connecticut Historical Society).

20. Root, *Character Sketches, Connecticut Daughters of the American Revolution*, 79–80.

21. Ibid., 85.

22. Brown, *The Life of Oliver Ellsworth*, 277.

23. Ibid., 82.

24. Stiles, *History of Ancient Windsor, Connecticut*, 602; Root, *Character Sketches, Connecticut Daughters of the American Revolution*, 84; Brown, *The Life of Oliver Ellsworth*, 340.

25. Root, *Character Sketches, Connecticut Daughters of the American Revolution*, 87–88.

26. Ibid., 86–87.

27. Brown, *The Life of Oliver Ellsworth*, 340–41.

28. Lettieri, *Connecticut's Young Man of the Revolution: Oliver Ellsworth*, 16.

29. Ibid., 16–17.

30. Flanders, *The Lives and Times of the Chief Justices of the Supreme Court of the United States*, 2:63. Flanders does not give the source of the quotation referring to Ellsworth's full docket.

31. Oscar Zeichner, *Connecticut's Years of Controversy, 1750–1776* (Chapel Hill: University of North Carolina Press, 1949; repr. Archon Books, 1970), 4.

32. Roth, *Connecticut: A Bicentennial History*, 73–74.

33. Collier, *All Politics is Local: Family, Friends, and Provincial Interests in the Creation of the Constitution*, 12.

34. Zeichner, *Connecticut's Years of Controversy, 1750–1776*, 4.

35. Richard Buel Jr., *Dear Liberty: Connecticut's Mobilization for the Revolutionary War*, (Middletown: CT: Wesleyan University Press, 1980), 58–59, 80.

36. Van Dusen, *Connecticut*, 144; Roth, *Connecticut: A Bicentennial History*, 83.

37. Lettieri, *Connecticut's Young Man of the Revolution: Oliver Ellsworth*, 19–23.

38. Ibid., 25.

39. Ibid., 30.

40. Oliver Ellsworth to Abigail Ellsworth, January 9, 1779, Ellsworth Papers (Hartford, CT: Connecticut Historical Society).

41. George Van Santvoord, *Sketches of the Lives and Judicial Services of the Chief Justices of the United States Supreme Court* (New York: Scribner, 1854), 205.

42. Henry Cabot Lodge, *A Fighting Frigate* (1907; repr., Freeport, ME: Books for Libraries Press, 1969), 75.

43. Brown, *The Life of Oliver Ellsworth*, 74; Lettieri, *Connecticut's Young Man of the Revolution: Oliver Ellsworth,* 33; Paul H. Smith, *Letters of Delegates to Congress, 1774–1789*, 20:191.

44. W. W. Abbot, ed., *The Papers of George Washington*, vol. 2, (Charlottesville: University of Virginia, 1987), 330–33.

45. John C. Ford, ed., *Journals of the Continental Congress*, vol. 12, (Washington, D.C.: Government Printing Office, 1904–37), 1064; Brown, *The Life of Oliver Ellsworth*, 67.

46. *United States v. Peters*, 9 U.S. 115, 136 (1809).

47. Ford, *Journals of the Continental Congress,* 14:1002.

48. Ibid., 15:1221–22.

49. Ibid., 16:61–62.

50. Ibid., 16:62n1.

51. Henry J. Bourguignon, *The First Federal Court: The First Federal Appellate Prize Court of the American Revolution, 1775–1787* (Philadelphia: American Philosophical Society, 1977), 116.

52. E. James Ferguson, *The Power of the Purse* (Chapel Hill, NC: University of North Carolina, 1961), 30–32.

53. Thomas Fleming, *Perils of Peace: America's Struggle for Survival after Yorktown* (New York: Harper Collins, 2007), 117.

54. Ford, *Journals of the Continental Congress,* 13:21n.

55. Ferguson, *The Power of the Purse*, 35.

56. Brown, *The Life of Oliver Ellsworth*, Appendix A.

57. Ibid., 76.

58. Smith, *Letters of Delegates to Congress 1774–1789,* 14:548–49.

59. Ford, *Journals of the Continental Congress,* 24:261.

60. Smith, *Letters of Delegates to Congress,* 20:413–15.

61. Gaspare John Saladino, "The Economic Revolution in Late Eighteenth Century Connecticut" (Ph.D. diss., University of Wisconsin, 1964), 196–97.

62. Casto, *Oliver Ellsworth and the Creation of the Federal Republic*, 29.

63. Litteri, *Connecticut's Young Man of the Revolution: Oliver Ellsworth*, 65.

Chapter 3: The Electoral Federalist

1. Elliot, *The Debates in the Several State Conventions on the Adoption of the Federal Constitution*, 2:200.

2. Richard B. Morris, *Witnesses at the Creation: Hamilton, Madison, Jay, and the Constitution* (New York: Holt, Rinehart, and Winston, 1985), 163–68.

3. Ford, *Journals of the Continental Congress*, 32:74; Alexander Hamilton, John Jay, and James Madison, *The Federalist Papers* (London: Penguin, 1987), 259–65.

4. Forrest McDonald, *Novus Ordo Seclorum: The Intellectual Origins of the Constitution* (Lawrence, KS: University Press of Kansas, 1985), 208–9.

5. For a summary of Madison's proposed Constitution, see the Virginia Plan in Max Farrand, ed., *Records of the Federal Convention of 1787*, vol. 1, (New Haven, CT: Yale University Press, 1966), 20–23. Although the Virginia Plan was offered at the Convention by Edmund Randolph of Virginia, historians attribute the drafting of the plan to James Madison. The consensus view holds that Randolph, then Virginia's governor, was selected to present the plan because, more than Madison, he was a forceful and confident public speaker. See Richard Beeman, *Plain, Honest Men: The Making of the American Constitution* (New York: Random House, 2009), 87–91.

6. Farrand, *Records of the Federal Convention of 1787*, 1:20–23, 282–93.

7. Ibid., 2:524; Forrest McDonald, *E Pluribus Unum: The Formation of the American Republic, 1776–1790* (Indianapolis, IN: Liberty Fund, 1979), 306–7.

8. Beeman, *Plain, Honest Men: The Making of the American Constitution*, 156–7.

9. Ibid.

10. Paul Leicester Ford, *Essays on the Constitution of the United States*, 176.

11. Beeman, *Plain, Honest Men: The Making of the American Constitution*, 157.

12. Farrand, *Records of the Federal Convention of 1787*, 1:485.

13. Beeman, *Plain, Honest Men: The Making of the American Constitution*, 87–91.

14. Farrand, *Records of the Federal Convention of 1787*, 1:193.

15. McDonald, *E Pluribus Unum: The Formation of the American Republic, 1776–1790*, 260; Beeman, *Plain, Honest Men: The Making of the American Constitution*, 59.

16. Farrand, *Records of the Federal Convention of 1787*, 1:193.

17. Ibid., 196.

18. Christopher Collier, *Roger Sherman's Connecticut: Yankee Politics and the American Revolution* (Middletown, CT: Wesleyan University Press, 1971), 3, 100; Beeman, *Plain, Honest Men: The Making of the American Constitution*, 114–15.

19. Casto, *Oliver Ellsworth and the Creation of the Federal Republic*, 38.

20. Collier, *Roger Sherman's Connecticut: Yankee Politics and the American Revolution*, 12.

21. McDonald, *E Pluribus Unum: The Formation of the American Republic, 1776–1790*, 290.

22. Collier, *Roger Sherman's Connecticut: Yankee Politics and the American Revolution*, 64.

23. Ibid., 236.

24. Casto, *Oliver Ellsworth and the Creation of the Federal Republic*, 38.

25. Evert A. Duyckinck, *National Portrait Gallery of Eminent Americans*, vol. 1, (New York: Johnson, Fry & Co., 1862), 337.

26. Flanders, *The Lives and Times of the Chief Justices of the Supreme Court of the United States*, 2:274.

27. Beeman, *Plain, Honest Men: The Making of the American Constitution*, 115 (quoting Pierce); Flanders, *The Lives and Times of the Chief Justices of the Supreme Court of the United States*, 2:66–67 (quoting Dwight and Trumbull).

28. Beeman, *Plain, Honest Men: The Making of the American Constitution*, 78; Casto, *Oliver Ellsworth and the Creation of the Federal Republic*, 38.

29. Farrand, *Records of the Federal Convention of 1787*, 1:201.

30. Ibid., 240.

31. Ibid., 322.

32. Ibid., 406.

33. Ibid.; Leonard L. Richards, *Shays's Rebellion: The American Revolution's Final Battle* (Philadelphia: University of Pennsylvania, 2002).

34. Farrand, *Records of the Federal Convention of 1787*, 1:407.

35. Ibid., 468.

36. Ibid., 469.

37. Ibid., 469, 475.

38. Bernard C. Steiner, *Connecticut's Ratification of the Federal Constitution* (Worcester, MA: American Antiquarian Society, 1915), 86.

39. Collier, *Roger Sherman's Connecticut: Yankee Politics and the American Revolution*, 253.

40. Farrand, *Records of the Federal Convention of 1787*, 1: 53–54.

41. Ibid., 255, 261.

42. George Bancroft, *History of the Formation of the Constitution of the United States of America*, vol. 2, (New York: D. Appleton and Co., 1889), 88.

43. Farrand, *Records of the Federal Convention of 1787*, 1:483.

44. Ibid., 484.

45. Ibid., 484, 496.

46. Ibid., 484.

47. Hamilton, Jay, and Madison, *The Federalist Papers*, 254–59.

48. Farrand, *Records of the Federal Convention of 1787*, 1:510.

49. Ibid., 511.

50. Ibid., 516.

51. Ibid., 526.

52. Ibid., 509–21, 524–37; 2:15.

53. The provision granting Congress the power to raise armies prompted an objection only from Massachusetts delegate Elbridge Gerry, an eventual non-signer of the Constitution, who sought to limit the power during peacetime. But Gerry's fellow delegates rejected his attempt to set constitutional limits on Congress's ability to conscript. (Farrand, *Records of the Federal Convention of 1787*, 2:329.) The detailed constitutions that Paterson, South Carolina delegate Charles Pinckney, and the drafting committee each proposed granted Congress a taxing power. (Farrand, *Records of the Federal Convention of 1787*, 1:242–45; 2:135, 167.) The proposition to grant Congress the power to regulate foreign and interstate commerce gained unanimous approval. (Farrand, *Records of the Federal Convention of 1787*, 2:329.) The delegates also fully supported the treaty-making power, disagreeing only over its execution. No one bothered to debate the prohibition that barred the states from negotiating treaties themselves. (Farrand, *Records of the Federal Convention of 1787*, 2:393–94, 540–41, 547–50.)

54. Farrand, *Records of the Federal Convention of 1787*, 2:193–212.

55. Ibid., 201.

56. Ibid.

57. Ibid., 203–5.

58. Ibid., 201.

59. Ibid., 248–49.

60. Ibid., 249.

61. Ibid., 213–44.

62. Ibid., 230–44.

63. Ibid., 1:361–62.

64. Ibid., 369–74; 2:290.

65. Gordon S. Wood, *The Creation of the American Republic* (Chapel Hill, NC: University of North Carolina, 1969), 517.

66. Edmund Burke, Speech to the Electors of Bristol, November 3, 1774, in *Select Works of Edmund Burke*, vol. 4 (Indianapolis, IN: Liberty Fund, 1999), 11–12.

67. Farrand, *Records of the Federal Convention of 1787*, 1:289.

68. Ibid., 381.

69. Ibid., 288–89.

70. Ibid., 290.

71. Ibid., 362.

72. Ibid., 287.

73. Ibid., 358.

74. Ibid., 408n1.

75. Ibid., 20, 291.

76. For Connecticut's political culture, see William Cullen Dennis, "A Federalist Persuasion: The American Ideal of the Connecticut Federalist" (Ph.D. diss., Yale University, 1971).

77. Farrand, *Records of the Federal Convention of* 1787, 2:219 (Williamson's motion). For the rule on direct taxation referred to by Williamson, see the report of the Committee of Detail in ibid., 168.

78. Ibid., 220–21.

79. Ibid., 364.

80. Ibid.

81. Ibid.

82. Ibid., 370.

83. Beeman, *Plain, Honest Men: The Making of the American Constitution*, 43.

84. Farrand, *Records of the Federal Convention of* 1787, 2:371.

85. Beeman, *Plain, Honest Men: The Making of the American Constitution*, 311–12.

86. "An Act Concerning Indian, Molatto, and Negro Servants and Slaves (1784)," in 1784 *Acts and Laws of Connecticut* (New London: Timothy Green Folder, n.d.), 233–35.

87. Farrand, *Records of the Federal Convention of* 1787, 2:371.

88. Ibid., 375.

89. Ibid., 374.

90. McDonald, *E Pluribus Unum: The Formation of the American Republic, 1776–1790*, 290–93.

91. Farrand, *Records of the Federal Convention of* 1787, 2:143.

92. Ibid., 307.

93. Ibid., 355–71.

94. Ibid., 375.

95. Ibid., 307.

96. Ibid., 375.

97. Collier, *Roger Sherman's Connecticut: Yankee Politics and the American Revolution*, 259.

98. Oliver Ellsworth to Abigail Ellsworth, March 7, 1790, Ellsworth Papers (Hartford, CT: Connecticut Historical Society); Casto, *Oliver Ellsworth and the Creation of the Federal Republic*, 50.

99. Oliver Ellsworth to Abigail Ellsworth, March 7, 1790, Ellsworth Papers, (Hartford, CT: Connecticut Historical Society).

100. Paul Leicester Ford, *Essays on the Constitution of the United States*, 164.

101. Casto, *Oliver Ellsworth and the Creation of the Federal Republic*, 50.

102. Brown, *The Life of Oliver Ellsworth*, 168n2.

103. Ibid., 165.

104. Edwin Percy Whipple, ed., *The Great Speeches and Orations of Daniel Webster* (Boston: Little, Brown & Co., 1914), 288.

105. Brown, *The Life of Oliver Ellsworth*, 175.

106. Farrand, *Records of the Federal Convention of 1787*, 1:335–36.

Chapter 4: "Landholder"

1. Casto, *Oliver Ellsworth and the Creation of the Federal Republic*, 56.

2. The vote was seven to three against Ellsworth's motion (Farrand, *Records of the Federal Convention of 1787*, 2:89–93).

3. Farrand, *Records of the Federal Convention of 1787*, 1:335.

4. Lettieri, *Connecticut's Young Man of the Revolution: Oliver Ellsworth*, 56–57.

5. Ford, *Essays on the Constitution of the United States*, 139.

6. McDonald, *E Pluribus Unum: The Formation of the American Republic, 1776–1790*, 304.

7. Elliot, *The Debates in the Several State Conventions on the Adoption of the Federal Constitution*, 2:190.

8. Ibid., 185.

9. Ford, *Essays on the Constitution of the United States*, 157.

10. Elliot, *The Debates in the Several State Conventions on the Adoption of the Federal Constitution*, 2:189.

11. Ford, *Essays on the Constitution of the United States*, 157.

12. Ibid., 140.

13. Ibid., 141.

14. Elliot, *The Debates in the Several State Conventions on the Adoption of the Federal Constitution*, 2:189–90.

15. Ibid., 191

16. Ibid., 191, 195.

17. Pauline Maier, *Ratification: The People Debate the Constitution, 1787–88* (New York: Simon & Schuster, 2010), 111–13; John Lukacs, ed., *"The European Revolution" and Correspondence with Gobineau* (New York: Doubleday, 1959), 78.

18. Max M. Edling, *Revolution in Favor of Government* (Oxford: Oxford University, 2003), 209.

19. Elliot, *The Debates in the Several State Conventions on the Adoption of the Federal Constitution*, 2:193.

20. Ibid., 2:186.

21. Ford, *Essays on the Constitution of the United States*, 190–91.

22. Ibid., 147.

23. Ibid.

24. Ibid., 153.

25. Elliot, *The Debates in the Several State Conventions on the Adoption of the Federal Constitution*, 2:190–97.

26. Ibid., 196.

27. Ibid.

28. Ford, *Essays on the Constitution of the United States*, 153.

29. Elliot, *The Debates in the Several State Conventions on the Adoption of the Federal Constitution*, 1:492.

30. Farrand, *Records of the Federal Convention of 1787*, 1:492.

31. Ford, *Essays on the Constitution of the United States*, 152.

32. Ibid., 164.

33. Elliot, *The Debates in the Several State Conventions on the Adoption of the Federal Constitution*, 1:492.

34. Ford, *Essays on the Constitution of the United States*, 146.

35. Ibid., 146, 157.

36. Ibid., 194.

37. Ibid., 141.

38. Lance Banning, *The Sacred Fire of Liberty* (Ithaca, NY: Cornell University Press, 1995), 116.

39. Farrand, *Records of the Federal Convention of 1787*, 1:287.

40. Hamilton, Jay, and Madison, *The Federalist Papers*, 156.

41. *Gibbons v. Ogden*, 22 U.S. 1 (1824).

42. Edling, *Revolution in Favor of Government*, 228.

43. Elliot, *The Debates in the Several State Conventions on the Adoption of the Federal Constitution*, 2:195.

44. Ford, *Essays on the Constitution of the United States*, 159.

45. Ibid., 159, 164.

46. Elliot, *The Debates in the Several State Conventions on the Adoption of the Federal Constitution*, 2:196.

47. Ibid.

48. *Calder v. Bull*, 3 U.S. 386 (1798).

49. Gordon S. Wood, *Empire of Liberty: A History of the Early Republic, 1789–1815* (New York: Oxford University Press, 2009), 447.

50. Reprinted in William Jeffrey Jr., "Letters of Brutus: A Neglected Element in the Ratification Campaign of 1787–88," *Cincinnati Law Review* XL (1971), 742.

51. Ibid., 747, 741.

52. Ibid., 772.

53. Hamilton, Jay, and Madison, *The Federalist Papers*, 436–42; Farrand, *Records of the Federal Convention of 1787*, 3:134.

54. William T. Hutchinson and William M. E. Rachal, eds., *The Papers of James Madison*, (Chicago: University of Chicago Press, 1962–77 (vols. 1–10); 9:348–57; Farrand, *Records of the Federal Convention of 1787*, 1:284.

55. Hamilton, Jay, and Madison, *The Federalist Papers*, 445.

56. Farrand, *Records of the Federal Convention of 1787*, 3:134.

57. Ibid., 1:293.

58. Ibid., 3:134.

59. Jeffrey Jr., "Letters of Brutus: A Neglected Element in the Ratification Campaign of 1787–88."

60. Gregory E. Maggs, "A Concise Guide to the *Federalist Papers* as a Source of the Original Meaning of the United States Constitution," *Boston University Law Review* (2007), 812–13; Appendix B.

61. Joseph M. Bessette, ed., *Toward a More Perfect Union: Writings of Herbert J. Storing* (Washington, D.C.: AEI Press, 1995), 77–107.

62. Ford, *Essays on the Constitution of the United States*, 191.

63. Bellamy, *Four Sermons on the Wisdom of God in the Permission of Sins*, 6.

64. Ford, *Essays on the Constitution of the United States*, 159–60.

65. Ibid., 196–99.

66. Ibid., 139–40.

67. Smith, Adam, *An Inquiry into the Nature and Causes of the Wealth of Nations*, vol. 1, (1776; repr. R. S. Campbell and A. S. Skinner, eds., Indianapolis, IN: Liberty Fund, 1981), 22.

68. Hamilton, Jay, and Madison, *The Federalist Papers*, 122–28.

69. Elliot, *The Debates in the Several State Conventions on the Adoption of the Federal Constitution*, 2:186, 192.

70. Casto, *Oliver Ellsworth and the Creation of the Federal Republic*, 55.

71. Hamilton, Jay, and Madison, *The Federalist Papers*, 318–22; Ford, *Essays on the Constitution of the United States*, 166–68.

72. Ford, *Essays on the Constitution of the United States*, 147.

Chapter 5: Court-Maker

1. Oliver Ellsworth to Abigail Ellsworth, March 8, 1789, Ellsworth Papers, (Hartford, CT: Connecticut Historical Society).

2. Farrand, *Records of the Federal Convention of 1787*, 1:119–25.

3. Ibid., 124.

4. Marcus, *Documentary History of the Supreme Court of the United States*, vol. 4, (New York: Columbia University, 1992), 444.

5. Abraham Baldwin to Joel Barlow, June 14, 1789, Pequot Papers, Beinecke Rare Book and Manuscript Library, Yale University; Kenneth R. Bowling and Helen E. Veit, eds., *Documentary History of the First Federal Congress*, vol. 9, (Baltimore, MD: Johns Hopkins University, 1988), 91.

6. Brown, *The Life of Oliver Ellsworth*, 185.

7. Marcus, *Documentary History of the Supreme Court of the United States*, 4:381–82.

8. William R. Casto, *The Supreme Court in the Early Republic* (Columbia, SC: University of South Carolina Press, 1995), 28; Lettieri, *Connecticut's Young Man of the Revolution: Oliver Ellsworth*, 28.

9. *Federalist* 80 in Hamilton, Jay, and Madison, *The Federalist Papers*, 445–50. *Federalist* 80 was first published on May 28, 1788. By then, eight states had ratified the Constitution. (Maggs, "A Concise Guide to the *Federalist Papers* as a Source of the Original Meaning of the United States Constitution.")

10. Merrill Jensen, ed., *The Documentary History of the Ratification of the Constitution*, (Madison, WI: State Historical Society of Wisconsin, 1976), 2:1027–34 (Virginia); 1034–38 (New York); 597–99, 623–25 (Pennsylvania).

11. Marcus, *Documentary History of the Supreme Court of the United States*, 4:54.

12. Ibid., 365, 535.

13. Herbert J. Storing, ed., *The Complete Anti-Federalist*, (Chicago: University of Chicago: 1981), 2:243, 315, 428.

14. Ford, *Essays on the Constitution of the United States*, 159; Farrand, *Records of the Federal Convention of 1787*, 1:124–25.

15. Marcus, *Documentary History of the Supreme Court of the United States*, 4:375.

16. Ford, *Essays on the Constitution of the United States*, 142–43; John C. Fitzpatrick, ed., *The Writings of George Washington from the Original Manuscript Sources, 1745–1799*, vol. 29, (Washington, D.C.: Government Printing Office, 1931–1944), 124.

17. Ford, *Essays on the Constitution of the United States*, 160.

18. Storing, *The Complete Anti-Federalist*, 2:243.

19. Wythe Holt, "'To Establish Justice': Politics, The Judiciary Act of 1789, and the Invention of Federal Courts," *Duke Law Journal* (1989), 1438–50.

20. Ibid.

21. Kate Mason Rowland, ed., *The Life of George Mason, 1725–1792* (New York: G. P. Putnam's Sons, 1892), 46.

22. Joseph Jones of Virginia represented the critics concerned with the material expense when he wrote his friend James Madison to remind the congressman that the new system of federal courts should not incur "more expense than is indispensably necessary for moving forward the great machine." (Marcus, *Documentary History of the Supreme Court of the United States*, 4:26.) Anti-Federalist pamphleteer Brutus captured the concern of having too few courts when he complained that without other federal courts, "no man of middling fortune" could afford to bring a case to the Supreme Court. It should be noted that Brutus believed that permitting the federal judiciary to hear cases in "different parts of the union . . . would only make the oppression somewhat more tolerable." Storing, *The Complete Anti-Federalist*, 2:70.

23. Smith, *Letters of Delegates to Congress*, 19: 593–94.

24. Ibid., 20:182–83.

25. Fitzpatrick, *The Writings of George Washington from the Original Manuscript Sources, 1745–1799*, 26:398–400; Smith, *Letters of Delegates to Congress*, 20:241n1, 242.

26. Smith, *Letters of Delegates to Congress*, 20:254 (property); 183 (prisoners).

27. Ibid., 20:181, 229.

28. Elliot, *The Debates in the Several State Conventions on the Adoption of the Federal Constitution*, 2:189.

29. Marcus, *Documentary History of the Supreme Court of the United States*, 4:498–99.

30. Farrand, *Records of the Federal Convention of 1787*, 1:492. For Ellsworth's perspective on the consequences of American disunity, see, e.g., "Landholder, I," and "Landholder, II," in Ford, *Essays on the Constitution of the United States*, 139–45, and the opening address he delivered at the Connecticut ratifying convention in Elliot, *The Debates in the Several State Conventions on the Adoption of the Federal Constitution*, 2:185–90. The *Hamilton* opinion is at 11 F. Cas. 336 (C.C.D.N.C. 1796) (No. 5980).

31. Casto, *The Supreme Court in the Early Republic*, 46.

32. Marcus, *Documentary History of the Supreme Court of the United States*, 4:409.

33. Ibid., 408–9.

34. Ibid.

35. Dwight F. Henderson, *Courts for a New Nation* (Washington, D.C.: Public Affairs Press, 1971), 77.

36. Ibid., 72–89.

37. Ford, *Essays on the Constitution of the United States*, 164–65.

38. Robert N. Clinton, "A Mandatory View of Federal Court Jurisdiction: Early Implementation of and Departures from the Constitutional Plan," *Columbia Law Review* (1986) 86:1515, 1517–18.

39. Marcus, *Documentary History of the Supreme Court of the United States*, 4:382.

40. Ibid., 25–26.

41. Ibid., 416.

42. Ibid., 422.

43. Henderson, *Courts for a New Nation*, 72.

44. Marcus, *Documentary History of the Supreme Court of the United States*, 3:401–7.

45. Ibid., 4:36.

46. Wilfred J. Ritz, *Rewriting the History of the Judiciary Act of 1789* (Norman, OK: University of Oklahoma, 1989), 38.

47. Storing, *The Complete Anti-Federalist*, 2:70; Maier, *Ratification: The People Debate the Constitution, 1787–88*, 287; Elliot, *The Debates in the Several State Conventions on the Adoption of the Federal Constitution*, 3:588.

48. *Journals of the Continental Congress*, 16:62.

49. Storing, *The Complete Anti-Federalist*, 2:320.

50. Marcus, *Documentary History of the Supreme Court of the United States*, 4:382.

51. Storing, *The Complete Anti-Federalist*, 2:434.

52. Marcus, *Documentary History of the Supreme Court of the United States*, 4:123.

53. Storing, *The Complete Anti-Federalist*, 2:429; Maier, *Ratification: The People Debate the Constitution, 1787–88*, 288.

54. Ibid., 435, 422–23.

55. Ibid., 436–37.

56. Casto, *The Supreme Court in the Early Republic*, 184.

57. Marcus, *Documentary History of the Supreme Court of the United States*, 4:495.

58. *Journal of the Senate of the United States*, 1st Cong., 1st sess., 42; Casto, *Oliver Ellsworth and the Creation of the Federal Republic*, 76.

59. Oliver Ellsworth to Richard Law, August 4, 1789, in Marcus, *Documentary History of the Supreme Court of the United States*, 4:495–96.

60. Ford, *Essays on the Constitution of the United States*, 159.

Chapter 6: Cases and Controversies

1. Charles R. King, ed., *The Life and Correspondence of Rufus King*, vol. 1, (New York: Putnam, 1894), 517.

2. Ibid., 518.

3. Connecticut Historical Society, Oliver Wolcott Jr. Papers, Series I, Folder VIII, 18.

4. King, *The Life and Correspondence of Rufus King*, 1:518–20.

5. Ibid., 523.

6. Connecticut Historical Society, Oliver Wolcott Jr. Papers, Series I, Folder VIII, 18.

7. Joseph Ralston Hayden, *The Senate and Treaties, 1789–1817: The Development of the Treaty-Making Functions of the United States Senate During Their Formative Period* (New York: Macmillan, 1920), quoted in Stanley Elkins and Eric McKitrick, *The Age of Federalism* (New York: Oxford University, 1993), 826.

8. Jerald A. Combs, *Jay Treaty,* (Berkeley, CA: University of California, 1970), 175.

9. Ibid., 176.

10. Marcus, *Documentary History of the Supreme Court of the United States,* (New York: Columbia University Press, 1985), 1:843.

11. Oliver Ellsworth to Oliver Wolcott Sr., March 8, 1796, in Flanders, *The Lives and Times of the Chief Justices of the Supreme Court of the United States,* 2:181.

12. Flanders, *The Lives and Times of the Chief Justices of the Supreme Court of the United States,* 2:182.

13. Oliver Ellsworth to Jonathan Trumbull, March 13, 1796, George Washington Papers, Library of Congress; Fitzpatrick, *Writings of Washington,* 35:2–5.

14. James Morton Smith, *Freedom's Fetters* (Ithaca, NY: Cornell University Press, 1956), 103.

15. Ibid., 142.

16. Julius Goebel Jr., *Antecedents and Beginnings to 1801* (New York: Macmillan, 1971), 646.

17. Marcus, *Documentary History of the Supreme Court of the United States,* 3:357–59.

18. William Blackstone, *Commentaries on the Laws of England,* vol. 4, (Oxford: Clarendon Press, 1765–69), 150.

19. Marcus, *Documentary History of the Supreme Court of the United States,* 3:358.

20. Ibid., 359; Casto, *Oliver Ellsworth and the Creation of the Federal Republic,* 117.

21. Goebel Jr., *Antecedents and Beginnings to 1801,* 646–47.

22. Marcus, *Documentary History of the Supreme Court of the United States,* 3:375–80.

23. Alexander DeConde, *The Quasi-War: The Politics and Diplomacy of the Undeclared War with France, 1797–1801* (New York: Scribner's, 1966), vii, 3–12.

24. Ibid., 74–108.

25. David McCullough, *John Adams* (New York: Simon & Schuster, 2001), 499.

26. Ibid., 523.

27. Ralph Adams Brown, *The Presidency of John Adams* (Lawrence, KS: University of Kansas, 1975), 97.

28. DeConde, *The Quasi-War: The Politics and Diplomacy of the Undeclared War with France, 1797–1801,* 181; McCullough, *John Adams,* 523–24.

29. DeConde, *The Quasi-War: The Politics and Diplomacy of the Undeclared War with France, 1797–1801,* 182.

30. Ibid., 185; Brown, *The Presidency of John Adams*, 100.

31. DeConde, *The Quasi-War: The Politics and Diplomacy of the Undeclared War with France, 1797–1801*, 185.

32. Casto, *Oliver Ellsworth and the Creation of the Federal Republic*, 117.

33. DeConde, *The Quasi-War: The Politics and Diplomacy of the Undeclared War with France, 1797–1801*, 185.

34. Brown, *The Life of Oliver Ellsworth*, 275–77.

35. Ibid., 279–80.

36. Jack Rakove, *Revolutionaries: A New History of the Invention of America*, (New York: Houghton Mifflin Harcourt, 2010), 259–60.

37. Oliver Ellsworth to Abigail Ellsworth, October 2, 1799; December 5, 1799; and April 19, 1800, Ellsworth Papers, Hartford CT: Connecticut Historical Society).

38. Brown, *The Life of Oliver Ellsworth*, 281, 312, 314.

39. DeConde, *The Quasi-War: The Politics and Diplomacy of the Undeclared War with France, 1797–1801*, 291–92.

40. Ibid., 288.

41. Ibid., 283–85.

42. William Vans Murray to John Quincy Adams, Nov. 7, 1800, in *Letters of William Vans Murray to John Quincy Adams, 1797–1803*, W. C. Ford, ed., in "American Historical Association Report for 1912," 358.

43. Flanders, *The Lives and Times of the Chief Justices of the Supreme Court of the United States*, 247–49; DeConde, *The Quasi-War: The Politics and Diplomacy of the Undeclared War with France, 1797–1801*, 338.

44. DeConde, *The Quasi-War: The Politics and Diplomacy of the Undeclared War with France, 1797–1801*, 331–40.

45. Ibid., 339.

Afterword

1. Marcus, *Documentary History of the Supreme Court of the United States*, 1:123.

2. Casto, *Oliver Ellsworth and the Creation of the Federal Republic*, 118–19.

3. Flanders, *The Lives and Times of the Chief Justices of the Supreme Court of the United States*, 259.

4. Brown, *The Life of Oliver Ellsworth*, 335.

5. Ibid., 336–39.

6. Casto, *Oliver Ellsworth and the Creation of the Federal Republic*, 84.

7. Reprinted in the *Connecticut Courant* (June 7, 1802), 3.

8. Ibid.

9. Brown, *The Life of Oliver Ellsworth*, 5.

ACKNOWLEDGMENTS

This book was born in the "academical village" founded by President Thomas Jefferson—the University of Virginia—where I first came across Oliver Ellsworth in course taught by Barry Cushman. Along with Professor Cushman, I must also thank J. Gordon Hylton for his wit and friendship, as well as the entire faculty of the Virginia Legal History program. It can safely be said that it took an "academical village" to write this book.

I am grateful also to Josiah Bunting III of ISI Books for entrusting me with this project, to Jack Rakove, Richard Buel, William Casto, and Jeremy Beer for sharing their time and insight, to the Connecticut Historical Society for assisting with the research, and to my copy editor Jennifer Fox for her patient diligence. Not least, I must thank my publisher Jed Donahue and editor Bill Kauffman. Working with both has been an absolute delight. I could not have completed this book without them.

INDEX

ISI Books is the publishing imprint of the **Intercollegiate Studies Institute**, whose mission is to inspire college students to discover, embrace, and advance the principles and virtues that make America free and prosperous.

Founded in 1953, ISI teaches future leaders the core ideas behind the free market, the American Founding, and Western civilization that are rarely taught in the classroom.

ISI is a nonprofit, nonpartisan, tax-exempt educational organization. The Institute relies on the financial support of the general public—individuals, foundations, and corporations—and receives no funding or any other aid from any level of the government.

www.isi.org